First Year
— *of* —
MARRIAGE

The Newlywed's Guide to Building a Strong
Foundation and Adjusting to Married Life

Marcus and Ashley Kusi

www.OurPeacefulFamily.com

Publishing services provided by:

 **Archangel Ink**

ISBN-13: 978-0692725184
ISBN: 0692725180

Disclaimer:

The views expressed here within are those of the authors alone and should not be taken as professional advice. The information presented here is intended for informative purposes. The reader is responsible for his or her own actions.

In this book, we share what we have learned in life and marriage, therefore if any of the information is perceived as advice, please take it as a grain of salt.

Your Free Gifts

As a special THANK YOU for purchasing *First Year of Marriage: The Newlywed's Guide to Building a Strong Foundation and Adjusting to Married Life*, we created a 12-Week companion action plan to help you implement the chapters in this book.

To receive your free action plan and join our email community, visit:

www.ourpeacefulfamily.com/12weekactionplan.

Dedication

To Ellyson and Emelynn, the greatest kids we could ever ask for.

Our family and friends who have supported us throughout our lives.

All the wonderful guests who have shared their first year marriage stories on the First Year Marriage Show podcast, and the readers of our blog.

Contents

Introduction

Many marriages would be better if the husband and the wife clearly understood that they are on the same side.

– Zig Ziglar

Let's begin with why we chose to write this book about the first year of marriage. We whole-heartedly believe that in order for a marriage to do more than just survive, to truly thrive and be fulfilling, it has to be built on a strong foundation. Just as a gardener must tend to his garden frequently after planting his seeds, so must we continue to grow our marriage after laying the foundation.

As you already know, we are taught core subjects like English, Math, and History at school; but we don't get a marriage skills course. Nobody teaches us how to fight fair in marriage, communicate effectively with our spouse, or how to handle the difficult issues that married couples have to deal with every day.

Adjusting to marriage is simply the process of preparing a strong foundation to help you build a happy, healthy, and fulfilling marriage with both spouses on board. Before you begin this process, you have to purpose in your heart to intentionally make your marriage the first priority in your life. Value this adjustment period in your lives. Give yourself and your spouse patience as you adapt to your new roles.

Use your first few years of marriage, if not the first year, as an opportunity to discover and learn more about each other.

All of life's twists and turns, whether there are children involved or not, often make keeping your marriage your first priority a challenge. Even with a busy life we need to purposefully carve out time every day to connect with each other. Seriously, every day you have to connect and not just talk about the day-to-day stuff like who is paying what bill and who is managing your kid's schedule.

We are yet to find a couple that gets married believing it will end in divorce. Rather, the divorce happens due to the compounding poor choices and the result of at least one spouse not being intentional with their marriage growth as a priority. Marriage is not easy. If it was, divorce rates will be very low or non-existent.

In today's world, the statistics indicate that not every marriage will last. According to divorcestatistics.org, the chance of a marriage lasting is about 50 percent. Married couples are filing for divorce every single day. Your marriage does not have to be part of those statistics; however if you and your spouse do not put in the effort, commitment, and hard work a marriage needs, you are headed for an unhealthy marriage. A good marriage is worth the work.

You might have heard, "The first year of marriage is the hardest for newlyweds." This statement could be true for a lot of marriages, but what is it that really makes the first year of marriage the hardest year? Is it the lack of better communication, different marriage expectations, different financial views, the marriage adjustments, sex or intimacy problems, stress, selfishness, etc.?

Building a strong foundation for your marriage with your spouse is a *must*. It is critical to the success of your marriage and determines whether your first year will be the hardest or not. If you have observed any successful marriage, you realize these married couples' went through that first year too and still have a happy, healthy, and fulfilling marriage.

It is possible for you to survive your first year without getting divorced, or making it the hardest year. As the saying goes, prevention is better than cure. A lot of divorces can be prevented. In fact, if you and your spouse are committed to spending the rest of your lives together in a fulfilling marriage, you most likely will not end up in a divorce. To do that, your marriage has to be built on a strong foundation.

Now imagine your marriage is a canoe on a lake. You and your spouse are each sitting in opposite ends, one in front, one in back. If one of you is paddling and the other is not, you will only travel in a circle. If you both paddle your own way again, you are not achieving any progress. Now, add in the wind and the waves of life and you are in danger of tipping over with one or both of you falling out. If you synchronize your paddling, you are able to progress and steer toward your destination and have a smooth journey.

Here is the takeaway, in order for a marriage to work, both spouses must be committed to creating a happy, healthy, and lasting marriage. Both spouses must be willing to go outside of their comfort zone, grow as individuals as well as a couple, put their spouse's needs above their wants, and be equal teammates. Working together in marriage is a must.

In this book, we are going to share everything that has helped us build a strong foundation for our marriage with you. This foundation has safeguarded us against a divorce since 2010. Because of this marriage foundation, we are able to enjoy our marriage, family, and life together.

We wrote this book for newlyweds who want to have a happy, healthy, and fulfilling marriage. However, engaged couples will benefit from reading it too as it will help them in preparing for marriage. We have also heard of many instances where couples who lived together before marriage or enrolled in a marriage preparation class still struggled in their first year of marriage; so even if you have lived together or already taken a marriage preparation class, you will learn something new from this book.

If you are not a newlywed or engaged, this book will help you become a better husband or wife. Married couples that are frustrated with their marriage have already experienced great results by practicing everything we share in this guide for newlyweds. We also show you how to build a foundation step-by-step that will help you and your spouse to practice the skills you need to have a fulfilling marriage.

We have used the strategies in this book to build a strong foundation for our marriage. Since then, we have been helping newlyweds adjust to married life and inspiring other married couples to improve their marriage through our blog and podcast (www.ourpeacefulfamily.com).

To get the most out of this book, download the companion action plan from www.ourpeacefulfamily.com/12weekactionplan. This action plan will help you navigate this book and put into practice everything you learn. If your spouse is not on board, work on it yourself.

We are excited to begin this journey with you, to show you what we have learned through firsthand experience, and what we have learned from countless other couples. You have the opportunity to build a strong foundation for the marriage and life you both want as a couple. Enjoy this process!

Coming together is a beginning; keeping together is progress; working together is success.

– Henry Ford

Chapter 1

From I to We

People spend too much time finding other people to blame, too much energy finding excuses for not being what they are capable of being, and not enough energy putting themselves on the line, growing out of the past, and getting on with their lives.

– J. Michael Straczynski

As humans, we never realize how selfish we are until we get married and have to put someone else's needs before our own wants. Sharing our life with someone can be a big adjustment; it was for us. When you get married most of those "I" statements change to "We" and "Us" statements. The fact of the matter is, when you are a single unmarried person you only have one person to think about, yourself. However, marriage changes it all; at least it should. You have now committed to spending your life with your spouse, so everything you do should be geared towards cultivating a lasting marriage. At each fork in the road you look through that lens and ask yourself, "Will this help or hurt our goal of a happy, healthy, and lasting marriage?"

You are now married to the person you want to spend the rest of your life with. Someone who will make you chicken soup when you are sick, someone who will share your deepest sorrows and greatest joys. You have to think about how your actions and decisions impact not just you, but your spouse as well. Even little everyday decisions like: taking an extra shift at work, what to cook for dinner, who to invite to the Christmas party, or even having a party at all, where you spend holidays, when you go shopping and how much you spend. There are plenty of places for this issue to come up and for you both to butt heads.

Go into marriage knowing you are going to have to learn to compromise and learn not to be selfish. Begin your marriage with an open mind. Go into your marriage trying to really understand where your spouse is coming from with their perspective and background. You no longer need to think about just your family, you also need to think about your spouse's family. What your families do indirectly affects your marriage.

Why should you change? Because selfishness hinders you and your spouse from truly becoming one. Selfishness makes it a lot harder to work together as a team. Marriage is not 50/50; if it was you could stay selfish. Marriage takes one hundred percent from both partners. You must be open to growing and maturing, leaving bad habits behind and becoming better individuals, working on your shortcomings and pushing the boundaries of your comfort zones. This is really hard to do for many people, but it is important for both parties to be committed to growing together and as individuals. Marriage has the ability to make all of us better if we work at it.

Before marriage, I was always thinking about my career goals, my clothes, what I would eat, events and places I can visit with my buddies, how I would survive, etc. It was always about ME!

However, after we got married, I had to change that mentality to how **we** *would survive. I had to think about Ashley's career goals and how I could help her achieve them, places and events we can attend together as a couple, what our meal plans would look like, etc.*

It was not an easy shift. It took me a while to adjust to all of these changes, living as a married person, and this new way of thinking. – Marcus

I never knew how selfish I was until we got married. If you would ask anyone who knew me before I got married, I think they would tell you I was a very giving person and not selfish. I was also an over-spender and impulse buyer.

We lived on an extremely tight budget and that was a huge adjustment for me. Marcus was not allowed to work for the better part of the first eighteen months of our marriage. I was working three jobs and going to school full time. I felt frustrated that I couldn't buy some ice cream or a drink once in a while, but we did not have the money.

During this time our finances were so tight we couldn't afford to have any personal money to spend on whatever we wanted. The lack of money and not knowing how we were going to pay the next bill was extremely stressful for me. Marcus took over paying the bills even though we budgeted together so I didn't have that stress on top of everything else. I still had a really hard time not splurging and buying coffee or things like that.

I had to start thinking about how the things I did affected both of us. That was a really hard lesson for me to learn. But it was worth it. – Ashley

In our first year of marriage, selfishness was one of the first struggles we had to adjust to. We had to realize that we were both selfish and purposely choose to change this behavior before we could learn how to properly communicate with each other. We did this because in order for us to communicate effectively we had to be willing to put the *I* aside and agree on what was best for *us,* trying to understand each other's point of view. How to see things as your spouse does is a selfless thing to do, not selfish. It is not that we were horrible selfish people, we just had to evolve in this new dynamic of marriage because we were not our own top priority anymore. Every decision made impacted the both of us.

How to Move From Selfish to Selfless

First, admit your selfishness out loud to yourself and your spouse. Say, "I'm sorry, honey when I reacted that way to you, I was being selfish. I am sorry I hurt you. I will try to do better next time." Admitting you made a mistake can be hard to do at first, but it gets easier over time. This usually lessens because vocalizing your shortcomings helps you to remember them. Hopefully, you can recognize the situation earlier next time and perhaps prevent the repeat of such offenses.

If you feel like you are having the same, or similar arguments, review them to find the root cause. If you get into an argument every time you go shopping maybe the root cause of that argument is the money being spent. If you argue about chores, maybe someone isn't feeling appreciated or the other person is not putting in enough effort. Finding the root cause of these repetitive disagreements can help you resolve them and understand each other better.

Another great way to change your selfish attitude is to start with the little things so it becomes a habit. Is it hot outside? Bring your spouse an ice-cold glass of something to drink as a small display of love and appreciation. Put your spouse first. Buy their favorite ice cream this time, next time you can go your way. Delay the instant gratification for the long-term benefits. Don't hide how much you spent or what you bought. These are simple things you can start with today to strengthen your marriage.

Eventually, and maybe sooner than later, you will come to a discussion where you both see things differently and reach a compromise. Your differences will help you to build a strong foundation and set a great pattern for the marriage you both desire. That being said, we are not saying your husband or wife has to deny their actual needs. You should both learn *to put each other's needs above your own wants.* If you both put each other's needs above your own wants, and take turns when it comes to certain things, it will help you to argue less frequently.

Resolve the small issues so they do not turn into big issues. Do not let your frustration build up until you explode or build resentment toward one another. Remember, you can't change anyone except yourself, so work on becoming a better spouse. Improve yourself and if you are in a healthy marriage your spouse will follow suit.

To become selfless instead of selfish in your marriage, you must deny that spoiled little child inside of you that says, "I should have everything I want when I want it and how I want it." Trying to control what your spouse says or does, or feeling like you have to be with them at *all* times, is not healthy. While this behavior eventually leads to bigger problems it can also alert you to insecurities within yourself that you need to work on.

Thinking of your needs, and standing up for your morals, is not selfish. It is healthy and it makes you who you are. You need to stand up for your actual needs, otherwise you are creating a very unhealthy relationship where you deny yourself completely and lose your identity. Remember, an empty vessel has nothing to give. The trick is learning to balance it all. Understand that you are now one team and everything you do directly affects your spouse. Compromise means to meet in the middle. It is not about denying one partners need, it is about learning how to be creative and loving in adapting a new or middle ground you can both live with happily.

What to Do if Your Spouse is Selfish

Dealing with a selfish spouse can be extremely difficult. That being said, have you thought about whether you are also being a selfish spouse? Sometimes one spouse's decision to become selfless provides the other spouse with an opportunity to also learn. Do not start blaming your spouse for everything they do wrong. Communicate in love and with respect. We will talk about love and respect in a later chapter.

Remember to be patient. It takes time and effort to change from being selfish to selfless. This will not happen overnight for either you or your spouse. It is about finding the balance in your marriage; it is about give and take.

Your marriage will not be healthy and fulfilling if one spouse remains selfish. Marriage helps us to become better individuals; in addition, a healthy marriage helps both spouses' to grow and hone their character qualities. It is very easy to think about *I* instead of *we*. However, the more you

think about *I*, the less you think about *u*
leads to being self-centered; which breeds
are on the same team, even when your spou
take, you acknowledge it and make plans to
not repeat the same mistake again. That's h
ceed in your marriage. Always look at yourself first. Maybe
it is a mindset change that needs to happen for you. We like
to step back and try to look at the big picture. What does
your spouse do that you appreciate? What are their good
qualities? Then we try to treat each other with love and appreciation. No one is perfect and growing does take time.

If your spouse's selfishness is affecting your finances and
trust, and if they are not working to change their habits, you
need to decide whether you want to stay in the marriage
without your spouse trying to improve. We have come to
points along our marriage journey where we had to stop
and ask ourselves that very question. Neither one of us was
threatening each other, we just had to take a good hard look
at our marriage and decide whether the occurrence of this
issue would make us happy. To be honest, we had to let the
other person know certain things were unacceptable for our
marriage to thrive and be fulfilling.

Comparison

Comparison is never good in a marriage. You should
never compare your spouse to another couple or your in-
laws. It is inevitable that you will compare your spouse to
your parents or close friend/family member. Just know that
comparison can be detrimental for your marriage. How
would you feel if your spouse compared you to their parents? Do your very best to change your thoughts once you

yourself comparing your spouse to another couple. It be tempting to capitalize on the qualities of another person rather than your spouse, especially if their habits are driving you crazy. It is important to recognize when you start comparing and stop yourself.

There was a time when I would compare Marcus to my friend's husband. I found myself saying, "I wish Marcus was more outgoing, more of a people person, better at surprises and gifts." Then I realized what I was doing. I saw how it was negatively affecting my view of my husband and so I worked on changing those thoughts when they would come up. "Marcus may not be as outgoing, but that's because of who he is and I love him. Marcus may not be surprising me the way I like, but he has come a long way. Have I expressed clearly to him the way I want to be surprised? Have I set him up for success? Maybe I need to send him a list of things I would love as gifts for him to have on hand when the occasion comes. – Ashley

Set your spouse up for success, clearly communicate your needs and desires, take your happiness into your own hands, and appreciate how far your spouse has come. Accept your spouse for who they are.

Equal Partners

What does it mean for two individuals to become one in marriage? Does it mean both individuals must change themselves in other to adapt to each other, or does it mean just one individual must change to adapt to the other person?

What if two becoming one means coming together to achieve your marriage goals such as having a family and a lifelong commitment to each other while accepting and celebrating your individual uniqueness, differences, and talents.

The intention of marriage should not be to complete yourself or mold yourself into the person you think you should be or your spouse wants. Rather, you and your spouse should compliment one another.

We believe that in marriage two complete and unique people come together, without losing their individuality, to build a bigger, better component than they could not build on their own.

You join together to become one for a bigger purpose. As the saying goes, two heads are better than one.

Two Becoming One

After getting married we are usually told that we become one with our spouse which represents the intimate and closeness of any marriage. Unfortunately, a lot of people have the wrong understanding when it comes to the two becoming one in marriage. Among married couples we have observed in our lives, we can see a majority of wives and husbands think they must follow their spouses against their own good judgment because they must *submit* to them. It seems they don't understand that they have an equal say in everything.

Traditionally, in the United States, men were seen as the figurehead of the household. Husbands were the breadwinners and wives were supposed to be submissive housewives who took care of the family. This way of thinking stemmed from thoughts that women were weak both physically and intellectually. Of course, there is often a religious factor too because many religious groups believe that wives have to submit to their husbands. This way of thinking skews the scales of how much each spouse's opinion and judgment is worth in the marriage.

We started our marriage with some of this thinking. However, as we learned, we discovered that our marriage wasn't going to work that way. We strongly believe that a husband and wife should be equal partners in marriage. Each person's voice and concerns are just as important as the other. If the wife is staunchly against something for her better judgment or morals, then she doesn't have to submit to her husband's *higher* authority by default because they can't agree. In the same way, the husband has equal rights and responsibilities. Usually when you have a difference of opinion, you will learn to compromise. You both give a little and compromise, or one of you will have to let the other have their way. Just because you get married does not mean you have to mold yourself into the absolute likeness of your spouse.

Becoming one with your spouse doesn't mean you are going to have the same opinions or beliefs about everything. It's an expression of the true intimacy marriage can bring.

Dr. Henry Cloud explains it best:

"Marriage is not slavery. It is based on a love relationship deeply rooted in freedom. Each partner is free from the other and therefore free to love the other. Where there is control, or perception of control, there is not love. Love only exists where there is freedom... Love can only exist where freedom and responsibility are operating. Love creates more freedom that leads to more responsibility, which leads to more and more ability to love... The requirement for oneness is two complete people." (Boundaries in Marriage)

These statements really put any relationship dynamic into perspective, don't they? You are free to be who you are while working together towards your marriage goals. You must be an individual with your own boundaries and opinions. You must also be responsible, loving, and respectful. It's not just doing things that you want whenever you want.

You must grow spiritually, emotionally, and intellectually in a positive way, while keeping your priorities straight. *For true love and total oneness to exist in your marriage, or any other relationship, you must both be free and complete individuals.* It's not all about you; your spouse has these same rights, freedom and responsibilities, and you need to respect them!

Sometimes you look back and miss certain parts of your life before getting married, your freedom and your whole world revolving around what you want and don't want to do. That is normal and it is a part of adjusting. We like to focus on what we love about being married to each other and how that trumps being single. Getting married does not mean you now have to spend every single second with your spouse. You need to give each other space and alone time. You just have to understand that certain things you used to do will have to either stop or be reduced.

For example, before we got married, I used to play soccer at least twice a week. I watched soccer just about every single day. After I got married, I had to reduce the amount of time I spend on my hobby. For you, it could be playing video games, hanging out with your friends, or whatever else. I still play soccer and watch some games, but my family time is priority. The good thing is Ashley understands how much I love soccer and encourages me to play every summer. – Marcus

If you feel stuck or you feel like you are not your own person it may be time for you to stand up more often for what you want and not be as passive. Express this to your spouse and see if they can help you find time for yourself to do something that gets you excited. If you feel this way often it would be a good idea to get to the root of these feelings. What is it you feel you are missing? Then, take a look at your marriage and see how you can make adjustments together to provide you some of that freedom. We create our own happiness.

When the two of you become one team, you can achieve marvelous things together. Married couples have so much more freedom in marriage than some people think.

Making jewelry or anything crafty gave me an outlet for my creativity. I was learning that I needed to work on me, just as much as being a mother and a wife. I had to grow as a person as well as a wife with my husband, while keeping him in the loop of how I was growing so we wouldn't grow apart. – Ashley

If we had not adapted and grown individually, then we wouldn't have much to offer in our marriage and family. We would not be able to help other couples, too. By growing as separate individuals in healthy ways, we grew closer to each other. We were able to share new things we learned with each other and enjoyed learning together.

Before we got married, I had a daily schedule and plan for each day that revolved around myself. From work to entertainment, everything was about me.

However, after we got married, I had to change my daily schedule to adapt to being a husband. I had to now purposefully and intentionally schedule time (outside of work and college classes) to spend with Ashley.

It was not an easy transition for me because I enjoy my alone time, but it was a part of marriage I had been looking forward to.

An example was when I had to learn how to improve my patience. I am a very patient person in nature, but after we got married, my patience was put to the test. There were some petty things Ashley did over and over again that tested my patience. I could not understand why she could not keep her wardrobe organized. It drove me crazy to look in her closet.

Over time, I learned what she thought was "organized," was completely different from my point of view. I mean, is it worth it to spend an hour arguing over how a closet should be organized?

By learning to be more patient and accepting her view on organization, we were able to prevent unnecessary arguments. As a result, my patience improved a lot which improved our marriage. It also became a skill that has served me well after I became a father. – Marcus

We realize this way of thinking is controversial in many communities. This is just what we believe should be the way a marriage relationship works, to be equal partners, with mutual respect. Each spouse's opinion has equal worth to the other. We believe this way of thinking is the healthy way to approach a marriage relationship.

A woman is human. She is not better, wiser, stronger, more intelligent, more creative, or more responsible than a man. Likewise, she is never less. Equality is a given. A woman is human. – Vera Nazarian

Marriage is about being on the same team. You both work together to achieve the same goals and you support each other in pursuing personal goals. When one spouse is lacking in something, the other picks up the slack. It is a give and take, hand in hand.

There will be plenty of discoveries of quirks, habits and pet peeves in your first year of marriage; so learning how to adjust is important. Having a change of mindset can help put things in perspective.

Marcus does this high-pitched screech thing when he is playing with the girls and it annoyed and embarrassed me. It was like nails on a chalkboard to me. It was him being excited and something I felt bad about being annoyed by it; because he was simply expressing himself and the girls loved it.

I had a pretty morbid thought. What if he wasn't here tomorrow? Would I miss this sound? The answer was a resounding yes. I would look back and see how trivial this was. It changed my entire outlook on this situation.

Sometimes we get caught up so much in our own little box of what is happening that we forget to look at the big picture. This is something that has helped me with parenting and reducing stress in general. I ask myself, is this really worth the stress? Will this really matter in an hour/tomorrow/a year? Is this worth my energy? This helps me shift my mindset about certain annoyances and opens my mind to accepting more. – Ashley

Your spouse loves and accepts you and you should do the same for them. Obviously disrespectful, hurtful, and addictive habits should not be accepted, but worked on and seek help when needed.

There is a great quote by the late Zig Ziglar, *"Husbands and wives would get along much better if they both realized they are on the same team."* It sounds like this should be common sense right? Why do you think Ziglar thought it was important enough to mention? Sometimes it can be hard when we are in the thick of things to remember this quote because we get emotional. Every now and then it is hard to remember in the heat of the moment that we are on the same team, that we both want the same goal: a happy, healthy, and fulfilling marriage.

Working Together as a Team

You have to have clear goals. Which end zone do you want to score in? Which play do you want to run? Have you talked about what kind of a life you want to create together? What kind of life do you want to live? What do you want your life to look like in 5, 10, or 50 years? These are the conversations you need to have to set goals. So you can work together as a team to achieve the goals you both set. We will get to these goals more in depth later on.

As husband and wife it is important to work together as a team to face the challenges life throws at us and to enjoy the good times in life as well. What happens when we can't agree on something? How do you remain teammates when you don't see eye to eye over an issue? Sometimes we have to agree to disagree. Sometimes we have to find a compromise. Other times we have to put our discussion on hold so we can both have time to better think it through. Sometimes one spouse has to give into the other spouse. An example of a time that you have to agree to disagree is politics, when you support Party A and your spouse supports Party B. There is no reason to let which political party you support bring havoc to your marriage.

We had an interesting conversation about this issue recently. We realized that there was never a feeling of a power struggle in our marriage because we are equals on the same team. Whenever one of us gives in to the other, we understand it is for the good of our marriage. We talked about marriages we knew where power struggles existed among the couples. We saw how it was hurting the marriage, pitting one spouse against the other. Never build your marriage on a foundation with a power struggle. Here is the takeaway: *you and your spouse are on the same team!* Having a clash of egos will not benefit your marriage. You have to learn how to be more open-minded and let go. Compromise. You should never feel like you are winning over your spouse or losing in a disagreement because you should both be winning.

As we mentioned, you will disagree with your spouse over something every day. You can look at something and have two different ways of fixing it. Most of the time, there is no right or wrong way for doing something, only your way and your spouse's way. Be open-minded to learning new things, looking at situations from another perspective, and appreciating your differences. Most of the small stuff doesn't matter and is easy to deal with quickly. When it comes to the bigger things we have to learn how to fight fair.

One way to help you grow as a team is to create a morning routine together. Start your day off together with a cup of tea or coffee in bed while you plan out your day. Share breakfast together, meditate together, go for a morning jog, or do yoga. The list of possibilities is endless. Whatever fits into your situation and routine, just include each other. If you absolutely cannot do a morning routine, create a nightly routine.

Because of our situation, Marcus gets up at four thirty in the morning to start his morning routine by himself, and then he works online. Whenever our girls wake up, he takes them down stairs to make their breakfast and give them their supplements.

If I don't wake up on my own by seven, the girls come upstairs and wake me up, and then it is time for his shower. I make his lunch and get the girls ready. Sometimes we have time to get a few things done before he heads out the door for work. I need this extra sleep and he enjoys his time alone in the mornings. The girls will wake up even earlier if I get out of bed in the morning because my youngest still nurses at night.

We do a night routine instead. After we get the girls to sleep we spend time catching up on projects we are working on together. This is something we both enjoy doing together, collaborating, and asking each other questions we would not have normally thought to ask. If we don't have time to work and connect, then we just spend our hour talking and connecting together. We usually go to bed by nine thirty together. – Ashley

Find something that works for your life and schedule and create a routine that fits for you. If you have highly demanding career, or opposite work schedules, it will put a strain on your marriage and the connection you have together. Make sure to schedule and dedicate the time to connect and keep your marriage priority number one.

"I have no way of knowing whether or not you married the wrong person, but I do know that many people have a lot of wrong ideas about marriage and what it takes to make that marriage happy and successful. I'll be the first to admit that it's possible that you did marry the wrong person. However, if you treat the wrong person like the right person, you could well end up having married the right person after all. On the other hand, if you marry the right person, and treat that person wrong, you certainly will have ended up marrying the wrong person. I also know that it is far more important to be the right kind of person than it is to marry the right person. In short, whether you married the right or wrong person is primarily up to you." – Zig Ziglar

Chapter 2
How to Fight Fair

Raise your words, not your voice. It is rain that grows flowers, not thunder.

– Rumi

Arguments and disagreements are an inevitable part of life and marriage. What is important is how we handle them. How we handle these situations will vary from one couple to another. Therefore, it is important that we handle them in a respectful and healthy way. Name-calling, yelling, belittling, aggression, low blows, threatening your spouse, constant criticism, bullying, shaming, intimidating, manipulating your spouse, humiliation, accusations, and abuse in any form are *not* okay. What you say and how you say it is key. In this chapter, we will show you how to fight fair.

See conflicts and differences as an opportunity to grow. You and your spouse are two unique individuals with two different backgrounds and mindsets. Disagreeing on something will happen eventually. When a disagreement does occur, you need to remember to treat your spouse with the same respect with which you want to be treated. You are not always right. Most situations don't even have a right way or a wrong way, just your way and your spouse's way of doing things. Remember, no name-calling, belittling, keeping score, rolling your eyes, or disrespect to your spouse.

The way my family fought growing up was anything but fair. There was lots of name calling, yelling and even physical abuse. I thought this was normal. I thought this was how couples fought. Unfortunately, I brought this expectation into my marriage.

When we had our early disagreements I was surprised that Marcus never yelled or said things he didn't mean like name calling. He would say, "I need you to stop talking to me and leave me alone before I say something we will both regret." That statement kind of brought me to a paradigm shift. Wait! We don't have to fight like this?

It was such a relief. It brought so much comfort to me knowing I didn't have to be on the defensive when my husband and I disagreed on an issue. It increased my respect for Marcus and helped us to grow closer. I was the hot-tempered and quick to react one, but I knew I didn't want this for my marriage. – Ashley

Sometimes, you need to take a few minutes to cool down and think through a disagreement by taking a break. Let your spouse know you need to cool off. Don't just stomp off and slam the door or roll over giving them the silent treatment. Silence will not accomplish anything but to create disconnection. Nothing will get solved. Communicating to your spouse that you need time to think and cool off is entirely different. You just have to say this statement to your spouse, "I am not ready to talk about this, give me some time to cool off."

I usually let Marcus know by saying something like, "I need you to not talk about this right now. I am not ready. Just give

me some time. Sometimes I can't even manage more then, "Give me a minute! – Ashley

One thing we do that helps with hot button or emotional topics is to ask, "Let me know when you are ready to talk about ____." This gives your spouse time to prepare and get in the right mind frame for whatever discussion you need to have. For us, we usually restrict the waiting time to twenty-four hours so the issues get dealt with as soon as possible. Choose a time that works for you and your spouse.

On days Marcus wants to go over the budget and my mind is just not there, I will ask him to wait until the next day. That way I can mentally prepare for it and save some energy. – Ashley

Think of the golden rule when communicating to anyone, but especially your spouse. It is common to see married couples who take their spouse for granted or have the wrong idea on how to treat other people.

Some things that helped us when we were having disagreements and were upset with each other were to ask ourselves, "Will this matter in an hour? Will this matter tomorrow? Next year?" Knowing that you will both be laughing together in the near future helps put whatever it is that you are arguing over into perspective. Something else we did was write down a list of at least five things you love about your spouse. Again, this just helps you move outside the situation and view your spouse through a different lens. Taking a step back can help show you if this is a silly disagreement that really doesn't matter, a miscommunication, or something you need to find a compromise over. In any case, it gives you a moments pause and a new outlook.

Communicating as adults with love and respect towards one another can help you not say things you don't mean because you are not trying to hurt your spouse. You don't keep score and you are not trying to one up your spouse. Mutual respect is so important in any relationship. You are both coming to the table to communicate which means both of you have the time to express your point of view, and also to try and understand your spouse's. You are equals at the table so do not expect to be treated any differently. Marriage is a hand in hand partnership, a team. You both deserve a say and you both deserve to be heard.

17 Tips for Fighting Fair

1. Never raise your voice. Ironically, we do this to be heard, but it only causes the one it is aimed at to shut down, or yell in return so they can be heard. No one is actually communicating and being heard when there is yelling.

2. Think about what you say before you let the words out of your mouth. You can never take the things you say back, so be sure what you decide to say is honest and respectful.

3. Palms up. Open your hands and turn them so your palms are facing the ceiling. This actually helps you to remain calm throughout your conversation.

4. If you feel yourself getting emotional with anger or hurt take a time out to think through things and calm down.

5. Practice empathetic listening. This way of listening helps you listen to your spouse while trying to see things through their eyes. Where are they coming

from? What makes them feel this way or think this way?

6. Find a compromise or take a break if it is something that doesn't need an answer right away.

7. Do not keep score.

8. Say you are sorry. Apologize when you are wrong and mean it. There is no shame in admitting you are wrong and trying to do better next time. To err is human.

9. Forgive. We all make mistakes. However, if this is a dangerous or abusive habit, then you need to seek professional help right away.

10. Respect your spouse and their opinions. It doesn't mean you have to agree, but you at least have to be respectful.

11. Do not involve other people into your disagreements unless you are both comfortable bringing in a counselor or a mediator. (Again, unless someone is abusive or doing something harmful.)

12. Limit the amount of time you spend arguing over your differences. If you have had this disagreement for a while and you have not yet come to a conclusion or you are either not making any progress or getting emotional, maybe it's time to take a break. Try to figure out the root cause of this reoccurring disagreement.

13. You may have little ears watching and listening. Make sure you do your best to model how you want them to expect a disagreement to be in their future relationships.

14. Try to explain your thoughts and opinions in different ways. We use diagrams, resources, words, and any other way we can think of to try to explain things so that we understand each other.

15. Have an open mind. You want your spouse to be open to your point of view, so you need to as well.

16. Commit to solving this problem. This tip is very important, as you do not want to have a pile of problems unresolved. If you are arguing over something that seems insignificant, maybe your argument is not about that specific thing, but what it represents.

17. Lastly, identify what the conflict is really about. It will help you to know which course of action is best to resolve a disagreement.

When I look back on those first couple years when I was so insecure, I see that I was unconsciously manipulating the situations and adding unwanted drama to our marriage. If I was hurt by something Marcus did or said, I didn't act like an adult and ask him what he meant by what he said or did, or explain what I thought he meant. That felt too vulnerable to me. Instead I put a wall up and would physically turn away from him, or act like I was leaving, or just go out of the room and wait for him to come in and make everything better.

He was so patient with me, but made his boundaries clear that he wouldn't coddle me. He used that exact word. Coddle. I reacted with, "Coddle? You coddle a baby! I am your wife!" Looking back, I know that is exactly what I was expecting from him. I put the responsibility of my emotional health and maturity onto him when in fact I was responsible for that.

I purposed to turn back towards him when I turned away until it stopped being my reflex. I intentionally made myself ask him what he meant when he said or did something that I felt hurt about. Sometimes it was through gritted teeth. Then I took responsibility for my own emotions. It was not his fault I felt rejected because he said he didn't want to go somewhere, or do something. Even when that came to sex (that was and still is a hard one sometimes). I started the long journey to overcoming these insecurities bit by bit.

When we feel something is off in our marriage, or not everything we had thought it would be, the first place we should look is within ourselves. I was expecting Marcus to fill every need for me and that is an unfair responsibility to ask of our spouse. We are all personally responsible for our own health and happiness. Our spouse should compliment us and other areas of our life. – Ashley

First, we must be respectful of our spouse and their right to their own opinion. We each have our own way of doing things because we are all different people with different experiences, knowledge, and backgrounds. Your differences can make your marriage great! Second we must be in control of our emotions. Know your spouse only has the best intentions in mind. Needless to say, you have to keep your insecurities in check here too.

Ashley's step-dad explained it this way:

"Opposite ions attract and make a charge. If you have two of the same ions, they won't make that awesome charge. In fact, they will repel each other. Just like in marriage, it is your differences that make you great together and keep that charge going between you.

You are individuals and that's the greatest strength you can bring to your marriage."

In our experience, a lot of people get so mixed up when it comes to marriage and losing their sense of individuality. You fell in love with your spouse because of who they are as an individual. Think back to what you absolutely loved about your spouse when you started getting to know each other. The truth is, it is usually how he/she compliment's your weaknesses.

One of the things I loved about Marcus in the beginning was that he was so organized; something I was most definitely not (although I have gotten a lot better!) I loved his wisdom about money and his willingness to work on himself.

This may not have all been the opposite of myself, but the opposite of the bad examples of men and relationships I have had in my life. It is one of the things that drew me to him. – Ashley

Before I met Ashley, I rarely did anything out of the blue. I was very organized and planned a lot. To be honest, I always spent a lot of time weighing the pros and cons of my plans. However, after I met Ashley that changed. I planned less because she loved to try new things, as well as be spontaneous. We both enjoy the thrills that come with it.

Being spontaneous was one of the things that I found attractive about her. – Marcus

Expressing a different point of view on something does not mean your spouse is rejecting you. Emotions are completely normal and part of our life. So it is important you can express your emotions to your spouse. If you bottle up your emotions continuously without a healthy outlet, it is a recipe for disaster. You will blow up at some point when you get angry, frustrated, and depressed.

I remember during the first year of our marriage when I was most emotional and insecure. Marcus didn't understand why I got so emotional over everything. "You don't have to cry," was a sentence he used a few times. I explained to him that my emotions are part of me. It's normal and even healthy to express them.

I used to bottle everything up inside and it took me to a very dark place. I told him that I would never do that again. Just because I was crying or getting passionate about something didn't mean he had to fix me. I just needed him to listen sometimes and sympathize with me. Other times I needed his advice. It was my responsibility to communicate what I needed from him. I now know to tell him when I need his sympathy or advice when moments like that happen again.

I have seen what not expressing emotions can do to a person and it's never healthy. – Ashley

The example above doesn't mean you have to be emotional all the time. It means you tune into your body and what your body needs. There are a full spectrum of emotions, not just sadness and anger. Your spouse should be the safest person you can come to and truly be yourself; while expressing your excitement, joy, uncertainty, frustration, etc. Your spouse should be a shoulder to cry on, a hand to hold through the uncertain times and through the exhilarating times! You should do the same in return. *As humans it is essential to express ourselves in healthy ways.* We need outlets. Sometimes we just need a good cry! Other times we need to get our aggression out and physical activity helps there.

You also have to be responsible with your emotions. If you are a crying mess all the time, or always angry and frustrated with your spouse, it isn't healthy. You get to choose how you react to your emotions. If you are getting angry during an argument, you need to communicate to your spouse that you need a few minutes to cool off. As soon as you realize your tone changing and voice rising, take a deep breath and try to calm down.

To fight fair we must listen to our spouse empathetically and try to see where they are coming from. Listening attentively to your spouse is so important for building your marriage foundation. Try to understand what your spouse means, why they think this way and where they are coming from. Listening empathetically means you are putting yourself in your spouse's shoes and trying to see through their eyes. You don't have to agree, but you have to try to understand them. *Do not* be thinking of your response while listening. This is a common issue when it comes to truly listening. Too many people listen to answer instead of listening to understand.

Fighting fair is all about disagreeing with respect. Sometimes we have to agree to disagree, other times we have to come to a compromise or give in to our spouse. Fighting fair is about finding the balance that works for both of you. We don't do this perfectly; sometimes we raise our voices and forget to take a break when things start to get emotional. The important thing is we are always trying to do better next time. Learning how to disagree is an important block in building a strong foundation for your marriage.

In order to fight fair, we must remember to think the best of our spouse. We must be willing to give our spouse the benefit of the doubt and believe they had the best intentions. In our experience, when you have an argument (and you will eventually have an argument) it is easy to lose sight of the fact that your spouse has the best intentions towards you.

I remember during our first year, almost right away, a lot of my insecurities came out. Insecurities I didn't even know were there. Every comment, every time Marcus didn't respond right away, or hear what I was saying, I would feel like I was being hurt and ignored on purpose. A big part of this issue was having to learn that we communicate differently, some words have different meaning to him than me, cultural differences, etc. The biggest thing was that I had to learn to overcome my insecurities and take control of myself by owning my emotions.

I had to remember to stop myself when I would start to feel bad, to remind myself that my husband loved me, chose to be with me and he means the best for me. Then I had to force myself to open up to him, which was excruciating for me because I felt hurt and turning away was my defense mechanism.

I would tell him, "This is what I think you mean, is this what you meant?" I would tell him how certain things he said or did made me feel. I would remind myself, he isn't rejecting you, he is busy doing X. He just isn't in the mood, he needs his space and this is something I need to work on. It was so painful and hard, but well worth the effort.

When I look back, I can't believe I acted the way I did. I was acting like a child. He was patient with me and created his own boundaries. He made it clear he wouldn't come running to get me when I would storm off in a crying upset mess. Not because he was insensitive, but because he was right, I was acting like a child who wanted to be coddled. We are adults and we can sit down and work this out like adults. – Ashley

Here is the takeaway; make sure you keep this statement in the forefront of your mind, *that your spouse has the best intentions for you,* especially when you are in the thick of things.

Keeping score in marriage can be devastating. It is also a form of manipulation. It doesn't matter how many times you did something for your spouse, or took the trash out. What matters is that you are both doing your part. We pick up the slack because our spouse is too tired to clean up after dinner or go to a social event. They do the same for us because that is how marriage is supposed to work, a hand in hand partnership. Keep this in mind: *your spouse never owes you.*

I remember I used to try to get Marcus to do things by saying, "You never do this." Or "I really want you to go so you can spend time with your wife." I really had no idea that this was a form of manipulation. This is how I got my way all my life; it's how everyone around me did things. I used guilt and I am not proud of my actions.

As soon as I recognized what I was doing, I stopped. I realized I had to respect Marcus's boundaries. When he didn't want to do something I had no right to manipulate the situation. I changed my attitude, reaction and the words I used. – Ashley

Let the angry word be answered only with a kiss.

– Thomas Hill

Chapter 3
Communication & Expectations

*To effectively communicate, we must realize that we are
all different in the way we perceive the world and use this
understanding as a guide to our communication with others.*

– Tony Robbins

Communication is the number one issue we receive messages about. It was also one of the biggest issues we faced during our first year of marriage for many reasons. As you already know, effective communication is one of the essential building blocks needed for a happy, healthy, and fulfilling marriage. In the first few months of our marriage, we simply could not communicate well with each other even though we communicated very well before saying, "*I do.*" It was a difficult time in our marriage, but we knew to have a healthy marriage we had to learn how to communicate effectively with each other.

By trying different strategies, communication skills and techniques, we were able to come up with seven simple and proven steps that have helped us to communicate effectively with each other without fighting.

Because of the success we had with these 7 steps, last year, we co-authored *Communication in Marriage: How to Communicate with Your Spouse without Fighting* to help other couples communicate better.

We want to share the 7 simple steps with you so you can apply them in your marriage, communicate better with each other, and build a strong foundation for your marriage.

7 Simple and Proven Steps for Effective Communication

1. May I have your attention please?

When you want to talk to your spouse make sure to let them know and get their full attention. If we can see one of us is in the middle of something we let each other know, "Let me know when you're ready to listen, I have something I need to talk to you about." Then we do just that. It is simple and it works.

2. No yelling.

Yelling will not help you get your voice heard any better. It incites different defensive reactions from your spouse all of which will shut them down. Stay calm.

3. A mile in your spouse's shoes.

One thing that we practiced was empathetic listening. This is where you listen to your spouse and try to see things the way they see them. Stand in their shoes and try to understand where they are coming from. It is not that you have to agree with them, but you do need to listen to understand them; then you can have your turn.

Recently, I had been looking at houses and land in the area. We are pretty sure we want to settle down here and talked about buying a house in the next 4-5 years.

I got excited and wanted to start pricing things and seeing what was around. An advertisement showed up on my Instagram for a real estate app. I quickly downloaded the app and searched this area for houses. I found the perfect house; it was $100,000 cheaper than what we had been looking at. It had almost everything on the checklist we made for our dream house and was in the town we want to be in. Perfect!

So, I got very excited and showed Marcus. I asked him to go look at it, explained how financially it made sense to me. We would be paying towards a house instead of the ungodly amount of rent for this county. He was saying, "No, I said no. You can go look at it, but I am not. We are not buying a house."

Obviously we hit a wall. I was passionately excited about what I wanted to be a sign and he was ardently against it. So I stopped him and asked him to explain why he doesn't want to go look at it or buy a house when I thought financially it made so much sense. As I listened to his response, I tried to see it the way he did.

He explained that his job is still a limited service position at this point, so he could lose his job at any time. We are not making enough side income to support us and pay a mortgage. Owning a house is a lot more responsibility. Plus we do not have our emergency fund built up enough to fall back on in case of a job loss, and then dealing with losing a house. We still have some debt to pay off and we need to get a bigger family car.

After he explained his thoughts to me, I understood how much stress this would put on him and us. I understood that this amazing thing could turn into a curse. I saw what he meant and realized he was right. When the time comes, we will find the perfect house for us (or build one). When the time is right, we will be able to buy a house and enjoy every minute of it. – Ashley

When it's your turn to explain why you see it differently, try to think how best your spouse will understand it. Be patient. Take a break if things start getting emotionally charged, defensive, anger, raised voices, snapping, etc. Of course, it will be different depending on the situation.

We believe as long as you are both being respectful and loving towards your each other, you can agree to disagree on most things. If it is something that needs a solution, a yes or no, like buying something or raising your children a certain way then you need to work together to find a compromise that you are both happy with. It may take several conversations over a period of time because such issues can be emotional, and to be honest, some issues require time and a lot of thought.

4. Confirm understanding.

You may be using the same words, but they may have different meanings to each of you.

For example:

Ashley called me silly one day and I got defensive and hurt. I wondered why she would call me a name like that. She seemed surprised that I was angry about it and asked me what silly meant to me.

In my country when someone calls you silly they mean you are stupid. She explained to me that here in the United States, it was not meant as hurtful at all, it meant funny or goofy. That was surprising to me. – Marcus

With us being from two very different cultures, there have been plenty of opportunities for miscommunications and misunderstandings. If you think about it though, you and your spouse grew up in different households with different family cultures. We learned to stop and take a breath when we felt offended or started to get emotional about something one of us said to the other. Then we ask each other, "What did you mean by that? I think you meant this, is this what you meant?" Explaining to each other how certain words make us feel, or what certain words meant to us has helped us tremendously with our communication.

Listening is such a huge part of communication. If you give your full attention to your spouse, ask questions to clarify, you will have fewer misunderstandings when you communicate with each other. Remember your spouse is not a mind reader!

5. Change your style.

Sometimes we understand things differently than our spouse. Trying to explain things in different ways can help get your point across. Using different words, examples, or diagrams has helped us many times to communicate our thoughts to each other.

We still have times when we realize we are both using a word, but that word has different meanings to each of us. It really goes beyond the gender differences because every person comes from a different family culture. In our case, geographic culture adds to it. That means that different words have different meaning to every one of us. It is safe to say that the majority of our arguments have been because of misunderstandings. Understand that your spouse is different and understands things based on their worldview of life. Try to be patient and ask them to clarify instead of lashing out.

6. Take a break.

When you feel your temper or emotions rising or you keep hitting a wall trying to explain or clarify something with your partner, take a break. After some time of reflection, you will come back calmer and with a fresh mind. Which will help you to make a better conclusion and understand with your spouse.

One recent example of this is when we had a disagreement over a project we were working on (this book!). Marcus wanted to scrap this chapter because we had written a whole book on communication and had plans to write another book on the subject of trust eventually.

He didn't want to be repetitive or make our reader's feel like they wasted their money. I was upset because I had poured so much energy and time into writing this book and was excited for the couples we could help by sharing our story.

I got upset. I actually threw the draft on the ground and left the room. I needed time to calm down and get a clear head. Marcus saw why I had left and waited patiently in the living room. (Patience will be so important in your communication too!)

After I calmed down enough to articulate some words, I asked him to help me with something and told him I just needed some time to calm down. When we revisited the topic we came to a compromise and realized we had been miscommunicating about the issue. – Ashley

Taking a break saved us from a big blow up and hurting each other while making a bad example in front of our children. Patience was key and understanding that we needed to take a break to clear our heads was okay. Do not think that just because you disagree on something your marriage is over. It is part of adjusting to married life. You are two human beings with two different and unique personalities.

*Unsafe habits like abuse, is always the exception to this.

"Listening is a magnetic and strange thing, a creative force. The friends who listen to us are the ones we move toward. When we are listened to, it creates us, makes us unfold and expand." – Karl A. Menniger

Listening empathetically helps us to understand our spouse on a deeper level. This also helps us from being so egocentric, thus changing our thought process from *I* to *We*.

7. Rinse and repeat

Take the tips from above and implement them over and over into your communication with each other and in other relationships.

These seven steps helped us learn how to communicate better and not fight like we did that first year. Since we discovered the steps, we have improved our marriage in many ways. For instance, when one of us needs to communicate our sexual needs to the other, these steps make it easier for us to share our thoughts with each other.

Lastly, communication can present challenges to your marriage. So take the time to learning how to communicate with your spouse. It will help you and your spouse to build a strong foundation for your marriage. We understand how uncomfortable it can be sometimes to try to communicate our feelings, especially in the beginning. *At the end of the day will you choose to love your spouse more than your comfort zone?*

Words are singularly the most powerful force available to humanity. We can choose to use this force constructively with words of encouragement, or destructively using words of despair. Words have energy and power with the ability to help, to heal, to

hinder, to hurt, to harm, to humiliate and to humble. – Yehuda Berg

Discovering Your Marriage Expectations

An expectation that has not been fully communicated is called a thought.

– Unknown

Expectations in marriage are one of the things you do not really learn about until you have been married for a little while. It is another one of those things you may be told about, but do not really understand until you are in the thick of things with your spouse. Expectations are needs and belief systems that have not been vocalized. We all grow up in homes that will always be different from our spouse's. For us, it was entirely different cultures as well.

You have to discuss the marriage expectations you both have because it will be much easier to understand where your spouse is coming from and what they are trying to communicate.

In my family the men are the ones who take care of the car stuff, oil changes, car repairs, tire changes etc. They usually repair stuff and do stereotypical masculine jobs. An exception to this is my mother who does absolutely everything she can, because she had to as a single parent.

In the beginning of our marriage something in my brain clicked. "Yay, I don't have to worry about changing the oil anymore!"

I quickly got aggravated that Marcus didn't know the first thing about cars. He came from a family that did not own a car, in fact a lot of people in his country don't because they are too expensive and a hassle.

I had to teach Marcus how to drive, change a tire, check the oil and maintain the car. He now understands what my expectations are and he looks forward to taking care of it. I didn't even realize I had this and many other unconscious marriage expectations; specifically these role expectations. – Ashley

Our environment played a certain role in our life and shaped our expectations in the way we each think about the roles a husband and wife should play. It is crucial to explore the way you each think about how you want your life to go. How do you imagine your daily life after marriage? How you will divide up the household duties? If you plan on having children, how will you raise them? Will one of you be a stay at home parent? How do you imagine each of your careers going?

When we got married I expected Ashley to do most of the cooking, washing the dishes, laying the bed each morning, laundry etc. I knew how to do all of these things, but in my culture it is usually the women that handle all of these. – Marcus

This may sound like we are a couple from the 1950s, so let us share some other expectations we had for each other with you.

*I had a deal breaker that any man I would marry **had** to view men and women equally. Just because I wanted to be a stay at home mother and he wanted to be the main bread winner, didn't mean we saw either of us having a bigger say in things.*

Equality in opinions and worth was an expectation of mine that I shared before we got married. Luckily, Marcus shared the same view. I expected to be treated as an equal, because that was actually the opposite in a lot of my upbringing. – Ashley

I expected Ashley to view life the same way I did. I thought we would be in agreement with how we dealt with our money, never borrowing or using credit. That was not the case. I expected her to see things through my eyes, and I had to learn that I needed to accept the fact that we will always be different; and that's a good thing. – Marcus

We had to communicate through our expectations and discover we both had very different ideas when it came to money, sex, duties, roles, how often we would be social and go out to do things, meet emotional needs, faith, resolving conflicts and so much more.

You need to identify what expectations you have, then have a conversation with your spouse. Communicate to each other not only what expectations you have, but why you have them. What do they mean to you? A good place to start is to think about what role your parents, or role models in your life, did or didn't do that you get aggravated when your spouse does or doesn't do. If one of you does not understand, take a break and revisit after you both had time to think about it.

Talking about your expectations is not a one-time conversation. You will have to communicate about your expectations and desires throughout your marriage. Usually, our ideas are very different in terms of how much to spend, but by communicating through them, we are able to find a compromise. Communicating about your expectations and desires is essential throughout your marriage.

A big contributor to our disagreements in our first year of marriage was the expectations we had for each other. These expectations of how we thought our life would go as well as the role expectations we had for each other were definitely a challenge to get out into the open.

You see, we all have ideas in our mind based on our desires and experiences in life. We may expect that our husband will take care of changing the oil in the car and filling the car with gas. We may expect that our wife wants to be a stay at home mom after we have kids, or that she will want to go back to work. We expect that we will go on vacations every year to a different place. We expect things like splitting housework, having separate bank accounts, spending money on what we want, eating the same foods we have always eaten, living in a certain house, etc. We have expectations about how we want our spouse to parent, how many times a week we plan to have sex with each other, how we want our spouse to react in certain situations, etc. However, most of these expectations have never been vocalized.

Think about how you picture your life:

» How do you want to be shown love?

» How many kids (if any) do you see in your future?

» What does your future look like?

» Where do you want to work?

» What do you want to do for fun?

» How are you learning and growing as an individual and as a married couple?

» How often do you spend time with each other's family?

» How often do you eat out?

» How much do you spend on groceries every month?

» How healthy do you eat?

Now ask your spouse how they see their life through these questions. Discussing the above list of questions with each other will help bring out some of your marriage expectations. Your conversation will help you and your spouse to have clarity about the future of your marriage. Which will provide a good structure for building a strong foundation for your marriage.

We have listed more than 100 questions in Chapter Eleven to help you both discover your unspoken marriage expectations.

Chapter 4

The Glue That Holds Your Marriage Together

Trust is the glue of life. It's the most essential ingredient in effective communication. It's the foundational principle that holds all relationships.

– Stephen Covey

You cannot grow together or connect with each other without trust. Trust is one of the important building blocks for the foundation of every marriage. In marriage, trust issues are caused through physical affairs such as extra-marital sex, lying, cheating, emotional affairs, social media, emails, contact with an ex, use of pornography, hiding money, spending too much, insecurities, not following through with your word, etc. Some of the consequences of trust issues such as infidelity can result in lifelong effects on your kids, spouse, and family.

Building complete trust in your marriage should be a priority. The lack of trust in any marriage usually breeds insecurity, leads to separation or even divorce. Being able to trust your husband or wife completely provides you with comfort, freedom to express yourself, and the ability to feel secure, less stressed, and safe. Learning to trust your spouse and keeping that trust going will require you being purposeful and intentional in your marriage. If you don't tell your spouse how much you over spent on something, or try to hide anything from them, you are betraying their trust.

Trust is the glue that holds your relationship together when there are times of uncertainty. We may not know what to expect, but when we know we can trust and rely on each other, it makes everything so much easier.

To build trust, you first have to be honest and sincere. Be open about everything with your spouse. You both chose to spend the rest of your life and commit to each other so you should be willing to work on being an open book.

From our experience, we know first-hand how uncomfortable this can be at times; how hard it is because of insecurities, stubbornness, and selfishness. However, it is for the best of your marriage. *Your trust for each other must be nurtured and protected continually.* As you go through the years of your marriage, you may get comfortable and take the trust your spouse has for you for granted. Just keep in mind that whenever you feel like you are hiding something from your spouse, it should serve as a warning sign. If you tell a lie or do hide something, tell them. "I was not completely honest with you before. This is the truth." Or, "I didn't want to tell you before, but I feel I was being dishonest and want to explain." It is always better to tell the truth to your spouse (unless you are in an abusive situation.) When it comes to building trust, you must also be respectful in how you talk to, talk about, and treat your spouse.

A great example of this is when Marcus and I were dating, but it still rings true today. When we were out in public and would go passed other women I looked at his eyes to see if he checked any of them out. He seriously never did. This was so important to me because most of the men in my life had issues with pornography, lust, and infidelity.

If he had checked another woman out, we may not be where we are today. I don't mean he never looks at another woman, but he never checks her out, no side gaze, no admiration of her body parts. Because of that, he earned my trust. I trust him to not have a wandering eye because I know that's the first step that can lead down the dangerous path of infidelity. – Ashley

We have agreed to talk to each other when we feel like we are missing something in our marriage, or when we feel like we may be entertaining thoughts of flirting with someone else, or even tempted to cheat. This brutal honesty is not always easy to hear, but it keeps us on the same page and it keeps our trust solid. We have always been very straightforward and honest with each other. We believe it has helped us avoid a lot of the marriage issues couples face. Sometimes it is uncomfortable, but change always is. We have to be honest to move forward in any relationship.

By being so open and honest with each other, we can mold and change our marriage as needed. We love our marriage and we understand that our boundaries are not for every couple. We believe that these are the basics that can help any couple that wants to improve and build a strong foundation for their marriage. Dr. Henry Cloud puts it this way, "Intimacy comes from "knowing" the other person at a deep level. If there are barriers to honesty, knowing is ruled out and the false takes over." (Boundaries in Marriage.) In order for us to feel safe enough to bare our souls to each other, to be naked emotionally with our spouse, we must be able to trust them.

Again, Dr. Cloud puts it this way, "True intimacy is the closest thing to heaven we can know." It's like one of the best perks we can have through our marriage. Truly knowing someone, having them know you, being truly loved and accepted for who you are and vice versa is so fulfilling.

The great thing about marriage is you get to create the life you want with the person you want to share that life with. You have the ability to mold your marriage and change the rules whenever you both agree that something needs to be changed.

In our first few years of marriage we were so unbelievably tight on money. I worked three different jobs and went to school full time. Marcus was not allowed to work while we switched his visa from a student to a green card holder, which took over a year to get sorted out.

I remember one of my jobs was at a small country store and when they had meat that wouldn't sell and needed to be eaten, the owner gave it to whoever was working. I also brought home broccoli stocks that they had taken the heads off for broccoli salad and were going to throw out. I asked to bring them home and I cut them up for us to eat.

We spent eighty dollars one month on food buying a big bag of rice, canned tomatoes and some frozen veggies because that is all we had. We were literally living on rice and beans. Marcus started selling books online that we had around the house, and then investing twenty dollars in buying textbooks online to re-sell. That was great, it started building bigger and bigger. He reinvested every penny he could.

Being in college to be an accountant, I helped him keep track of his books. I remember this one month the numbers were not matching up. We talked about it while we went for a walk and he told me he borrowed money from our checking account to invest in the books because he knew he could make it back with interest. He did do just that, but he didn't talk to me before tak-

ing the money. We sat down and budgeted together, I had to talk to him before I spent anything at all, so finding out he didn't even run this by me really hurt. I felt like trust had been broken. I explained how I felt to him and he saw how much it hurt me. He promised to not do it again.

It did happen once more. I explained to him that I felt like I couldn't trust him and I would not be in a marriage where I couldn't trust my spouse. I told him I completely understood why he did it. I just wanted him to run it by me. I run everything by him. It seemed to sink in better that time and he agreed about how he broke that trust. Since then, it has not happened again and he has not breached my trust at all.

As much as I love my husband and as much as he loves me, we both have boundaries. If these deal breakers were not respected by each other and neither of us were willing to compromise, we would have to end our marriage because it would not be a healthy and fulfilling one. – Ashley

"Deception damages a relationship. The act of lying is much more damaging than the things that are being lied about, because lying undermines the knowing of one another and the connection itself...Deception is the one thing that cannot be worked through because it denies the problem." – Dr. Henry Cloud.

In the second year of our marriage, I remember using some of our money to buy items to flip on Amazon without the consent of Ashley. I thought I was doing the right thing since all the profits I made came right into our account and was used to pay bills. I continued doing this for a while until Ashley was helping me do the accounting for the business. She saw the math and asked me where this extra money had come from. I was honest with her. Even though I had good intentions, she was not happy at all that I didn't talk to her about it first.

I was really saddened to know how I had hurt her and betrayed her trust. We were so tight on money and talked about every penny we spent, this shouldn't have been an exception. I learned my lesson and from then on, I always communicate with her before I spend any money we have even if I will make 1000X profit margin. – Marcus

That's one of the reasons it is so important to set these boundaries up in the beginning of your marriage and talk about them before marriage. Our boundaries and opinions may change about certain things throughout our marriage as well, so it's that much more important to keep your spouse on the same page with you about everything.

Infidelity and other major loss of trust do not usually happen overnight, it is the small compromises you make on a daily basis. Before you know it those small compromises, little white lies, secret credit card, or confiding in a co-worker can turn into major violations and loss of trust with feelings of betrayal. Setting up boundaries and being honest with your spouse even when it is uncomfortable will help safeguard your marriage.

Trusting each other is what keeps you together when the tough and uncertain times come. Without trust, you cannot have a happy, healthy, and fulfilling marriage.

In marriage, we have the opportunity to have the most intimate relationship with another human being, our spouse. In order to be so closely connected, we must bare our souls to each other.

Think the Best of Your Spouse

Why wouldn't we always think the best of our spouse if we love each other? When you have an argument it is really easy to lose sight of the fact that your spouse has the best intentions towards you.

I remember that first year, almost right away; a lot of my insecurities came out. Insecurities I didn't even know were there. Every comment, every time Marcus didn't respond right away, or hear what I was saying, I would feel like I was being hurt and ignored on purpose.

A big part of this situation was learning that we communicate differently; some words have different meaning to him than me, cultural differences, etc.

The biggest thing that I had to learn was to overcome my insecurities and take control of myself by owning my emotions. I had to remember to stop myself when I would start to feel bad, to remind myself that my husband loved me, chose to be with me and he means the best for me. Then I had to force myself to open up to him, which was excruciating for me because I felt hurt, and turning away was my defense mechanism.

I would tell him, "This is what I think you mean, is this what you meant?" I would tell him how certain things he said or did made me feel. I would remind myself, he isn't rejecting you, he is busy doing X, he just isn't in the mood, he needs his space, this is something I need to get over.

It was so painful and hard, but well worth all the effort I put in. I look back and can't believe I acted the way I did. He made it clear he wouldn't come running to get me when I would storm off in a crying upset mess. – Ashley

Here is the takeaway: make sure you keep it in the forefront of your mind, especially when you are in the thick of things, that your spouse has the best intentions for you.

A marriage without trust is like a car without gas, you can stay in it as long as you want but it won't go anywhere.

– Unknown

Chapter 5
Your Money and Your Marriage

Beware of little expenses. A small leak will sink a great ship.
– Benjamin Franklin

Money is such an important topic because it is the number one cause of many divorces. Due to this fact, we worked very hard on being on the same page when it came to money during our first year of marriage. To be honest, agreeing about money in marriage can be tricky at first.

Going into marriage you may think that your spouse has the same ideas when it comes to how much you spend on groceries each month, how much is too much to spend on an outfit, or a hobby. But always remember that you were both raised in very different family cultures.

When we started talking about money, we realized how different our mindsets were. Marcus comes from a culture and family that lives without debt. I come from a culture so deeply in debt and was raised to believe it was normal to have credit cards, car loans, and even loans on furniture. – Ashley

Now think about what you do with money. Do you save it? How do you spend it? Do you see any similarities or differences in how you handle money than your parental figure? How is it different? Of course we talked about money before we got married, but actually being married and discussing it was very different.

How to Budget

Knowing where your hard-earned money is spent is very essential for every marriage. Budgeting may be hard to do at first, but the time spent will be worth it. Sit down and write down how much income you expect to earn and receive during the month. Then, write down the bills you have to pay in order of importance. If you give any charitable contributions, make sure that is on the budget. Make sure your savings is on that list as well. Discuss what you will do if you have any extra money like paying off debt, investing, saving for something specific, etc. It is also important that you each have personal money that you can spend however you wish, just agree on a set amount and keep that money separate. By having personal money to spend on yourself. that you keep separate in cash, it helps keep you both stay in budget.

A budget will help you to direct where your money goes and how you will spend it before it disappears. As a married couple, it is essential you create a simple budget that will help you and your spouse achieve your financial goals. Even if you don't combine your finances, having a family budget for your money is a must! The tricky part at first might be coming to an agreement on how much you spend on things like groceries, eating out, entertainment, savings, clothes, and other things you want every month.

When you are creating your budget together, make sure you practice empathetic listening so you can understand each other's budget needs. Remember, you both have an equal say in everything that goes on your budget. In addition, you will both have to learn to compromise. Your spouse might want item X in the budget but you might not agree item X should be included in the budget or allotted such an amount. Before you make a decision, you first need to put yourself in their shoes to understand why they believe they need the item or have that much money put towards something.

Once you have a base budget done, (the items you spend money on every month) you will be able to tweak it and make changes as needed every month. Not every month will be the same. Some months have holidays and birthdays, so fitting everything into the budget will actually take a lot of stress out of your marriage. Keep this in mind: your budget will change over time as a result of life being unpredictable. Changes to your education, career, and income will all affect your ever-changing budget.

In our experience, combining bank accounts has had positive results for our marriage. It has forced us to have some important and difficult money conversations. We would not have had these conversations if our finances were not combined. In addition, our communication with each other has improved immensely. As a result, we recommend couples do combine their finances. By combining accounts all your money stays together. It helps you to both be on the same page. Your money is no longer just *mine* but *ours*. Remember, your personal money to spend should be separate from this account, or kept in cash on you.

We know that combining finances might not work for every couple. Do what is best for your marriage. For example, an exception to combining money is if your spouse has a gambling or other addiction problem that negatively impact's your marriage; or you happen to be one of the few couples that keeping your money separate works well for. Even if you do not combine your money, it is that much more important to budget together.

Why is it so important to have both of you participating in your finances? First, there shouldn't be any surprises like credit cards or any debt that gets racked up without both of you knowing. Another reason is that it helps you both be on track for the financial goals that you need to make for your family. Do you want to buy a house? How much down would you like to be able to put on that house? Do you want to pay off your debt? Do you want to be able to pay cash for your next car? Do you want to go back to school? Have children? Go on a vacation? Travel the world one country at a time? Be able to retire early? Then create a plan together! These are some of the reasons *why* it's important you create a budget and stick to it. These things don't just happen without a plan. The budget is your plan. The budget will be your friend that you have a love/hate relationship with.

*Marcus introduced me to a financial radio show by Dave Ramsey. I will admit, I initially thought he was crazy for thinking someone could pay cash for a car, or even a house! Then I listened to **real** people call in and share their stories of their journey to freedom from debt. After we got married we read Dave's book, "The Total Money Makeover", and it was like a paradigm shift for me. It felt **good** having a $1500 emergency fund instead of a credit card.*

The first two years we had a lot of things go wrong, and unexpected things did happen. Without that money we had saved we would have been in trouble. – Ashley

In summary, a monthly budget will help you and your spouse to:

» Improve your communication skills.

» Be on the same page financially.

» Set financial goals and work towards achieving them together by keeping you both focused.

» Identify places you are not spending your money wisely.

» Become financially disciplined.

» Reduces your chances of having money fights and problems.

» Reduces money stress.

» Helps you plan ahead for emergencies, or your life goals.

» Learn to work together as a team.

» Connect and grow together in your marriage.

Marriage and finances go hand in hand! Do not complicate things when it comes to creating your monthly budget. Keep it simple, and stick to it.

A Yearly Estimated Budget

Another thing we do is at the end of the every year we budget for the next year. We sit down together and brainstorm about the possible expenses that might occur for the year. We then budget for each expense to have a better understanding on our yearly expenses.

For example, every year, we have to renew our term life insurance, plan our kid's birthday parties, attend birthday parties, weddings, and holidays, buy new clothes, kitchen equipment, and upgrade cell phones. We also stock up on meat from our local farmers and put our bulk orders in for our pantry.

By doing this simple yearly budget, we are able to estimate how much extra money we need to earn for the next year and brainstorm things we can do to earn this extra money. When you and your spouse are in agreement on how you will spend your money, and what goes on your monthly budget, you are more likely to have a healthy, happy, and successful marriage.

An Emergency Fund

Besides the importance of budgeting together, saving is just as important; if not more important. We have an emergency fund, which we never touch unless it is an emergency. This fund has helped us from going into debt countless times, and also provided us with a sense of security.

For many years, our income was not steady. Our emergency fund relieved us of the money stress many couples have. For example, when our washer broke, we simply went shopping for a great used one because we had an emergency fund. Instead of buying a custom color brand new set, we used cash for an older used one that was still in great condition. By using cash, we felt every dollar that we spent which helped us spend as little as we could for the best value we could get. When we had a month with no income, we were able to pay all our bills on time and not have additional stress simply because we had an emergency fund. We strongly believe your marriage would benefit from having an emergency fund too.

Agreeing together on money may not happen overnight. It took me a while to come to my senses and agree with this way of thinking. Marcus was patient and compromised with me through this learning curve. Once I saw it working, paying off our small debts, having that security of an emergency fund instead of a credit card, I was sold!

It was worth it because in the most financially stressful time of our marriage, having this emergency fund took so much of that stress off our shoulders. I get really stressed when it comes to money and not having enough of it. The first few times we needed to dip into our emergency fund made it all worth it. I still struggle to stay in the budget, but the important thing is I make it a priority to try my hardest. I try to find ways to save or stock up on things when we have the money. – Ashley

Like many couples, we have had our own share of money fights. It was not fun, but we worked through them. Here is the takeaway; *we learned how to prevent ourselves from arguing over money by empathetically listening, thinking logically and making a plan.* It was not easy but it made us better as a couple.

When it comes to talking about money, it can sometimes be even harder than talking about sex. Don't let money be the reason why your marriage ends.

Patience is key when talking about money together. Try to understand where your spouse is coming from and find a way to compromise so you can both be happy. This is the best way to have your money talks. Financial stress is one of the most common reasons why marriages end in divorce. That alone shows why it is so important to be on the same page financially, as it is critical to the success of your marriage. No matter how much money you have or earn, you need to handle your money well. Money plays a big role in almost everything we do. Therefore as married couples, especially newlyweds, find a way to compromise and be on the same page with your money. Being on the same page and having discussions with your spouse will help you make better decisions together when you want to buy a new couch, car, where you take your vacation, and so much more.

Living in unity in our marriage finances has been an integral part of our marriage. It ensures we are on the same page on how we spend our money and where it is spent.

Write down each of what you expect to pay for things separately like food, spending money, electric, rent, supplements, etc. Then compare notes to see how your expectations differ. There are more questions listed in chapter eleven to help you both get on the same page financially with your monetary expectations.

At the end of each year we talk about the goals we have for the following year, which big-ticket items we want to buy, and how much we expect to spend on them. We plan out the big purchases and the smaller items we want to get to make sure we are on the same page.

Should You Live in Debt or be Debt-Free?

The thought of living debt-free was a hard concept for me. I was taught that everyone borrows student loans in college; everyone has credit cards for emergencies. These statements are not facts though. I've since learned how to live without these things and I cannot wait to pay off our debt. – Ashley

In Ghana, living with debt is not a common lifestyle. So discovering that many people in the US have debt in one form or the other was shocking to me when I first arrived here. I soon realized it's due to how easy and simply debt can be accumulated

for various reasons. I personally do not want to live in debt because it hinders me from many opportunities and plays a big role in making financial decisions. – Marcus

We had to talk about whether being debt free was a goal for us or not and this comes back to the life goals we talked about before. Would being in debt help your marriage goals or hinder them? Are we perfect? Heck no! It's been a learning process for us. One of us is a saver and the other being a spender. We had to learn our differences, discover how to work together, before finally agreeing on our finances. By agreeing on how to spend our money early on, we were able to build a strong foundation for our marriage. Always remember, agreeing on finances in marriage, and a monthly budget with your spouse is very important for the success of your marriage.

8 Steps to Creating a Monthly Budget

Step 1

Sit down with open minds and begin the process of doing your monthly family budget. Discuss why you need one for your marriage or family and the benefits of having a budget. Talk about something fun that you want to do, and your end goal. This is where being debt free, buying a house, traveling, and retiring early comes in.

Step 2

Identify all your sources of income for the month, whether it's from working full time, a part time business, donations, etc.

Step 3

Write down everything that needs to be paid or bought during the month in order of importance (your monthly expenses.) Make sure you include everything you both need for a month. Don't forget to add savings! Then write down what you would do with any extra cash that might be left over, like saving up for your next vacation, paying off student loans, credit cards, mortgage, etc. If you realize your expenses exceed the income you earn each month, eliminate some of your expenses so you have a balanced budget.

Step 4

Agree or compromise on every item on your budget. This is where your patience, listening, and communication skills will come in handy. Your first meeting will probably be the hardest and longest. After that, it will get easier.

Step 5

If you decide to have personal spending money, take it out in cash so you don't overspend. It is helpful to use cash only at first to help you stay in budget. When the cash envelope is empty, you know you are done spending for that month. Obviously with bills you pay online, you can use a check or debit card.

Step 6

Know that your budget won't be perfect every month. We all make mistakes. We can only try better next time and keep it a priority.

Step 7

Have a check-up, visual aid, or budgeting app so you can both see where you are throughout the month. I would suggest every week or two weeks you go over what is paid and what isn't paid yet during the beginning of that week. By having this visual aid, your children will learn how to create their own budgets when they begin to earn some income. We keep a white board right in our kitchen so we can both see where we are at on any given day.

Step 8

The next month, use the same base budget and adjust where necessary. Maybe you need more for one column, less for another, or a whole new column for an event in the next month like a birthday, wedding, or holiday which will require some extra money.

You can also use regular envelopes for each item on your monthly budget list. Each envelope should be for a specific thing in your budget. All you need to do is fill up each envelope with the amount of money allocated for it. Once the money runs out it means you should not make any purchases related to that envelope for the rest of the month.

By doing a budget and agreeing on finances together, you will connect with each other in ways you never imagined. The process of coming up with a budget and agreeing on finances with your spouse sets you up to work, and grow together towards your financial goals while increasing marriage intimacy. In addition, it will open lines of communication that would not be there otherwise. Being united over money will help you build a strong foundation for your marriage!

Remember, your finances can make or break your marriage. Never keep financial secrets hoping to reveal it later; it will not make things better.

Chapter 6
Sexual Intimacy & Spirituality

Anyone who is in love is making love the whole time, even when they're not. When two bodies meet, it is just the cup overflowing. They can stay together for hours, even days. They begin the dance one day and finish it the next, or—such is the pleasure they experience—they may never finish it. No eleven minutes for them.

— Paulo Coelho, Eleven Minutes

Sex can be absolutely amazing in marriage. Just like everything else in marriage; it takes intentionality. When you are married for any length of time, you know that we go through different seasons in our life when it comes to our sexual needs and wants. It is important that you and your spouse keep the conversation about your sex life going throughout your marriage. What you may like today, you may not like tomorrow. How often you want to make love may also change throughout your life. Despite sex being one of the most important ingredients to a successful marriage, a simple conversation about sex can be hard for some couples at first. Just like anything we do, with practice it gets easier. In the same way, having honest, sincere and frank discussions with your spouse about sex will get easier.

Talk about what you don't like when you are not in the bedroom. "Honey, I really get turned off when this happens, but I really loved when you did this". To do that, it is important to know that your spouse cannot read your mind when it comes to the bedroom any more than in the rest of your marriage. You are going to have to tell and show them what you like. They will have to do the same. Ask questions like: "Do you like it better when I do this, or this?"

We are sure you have heard the saying; *Sex starts in the kitchen.* It is so important to connect throughout the day. Let your spouse know you are thinking of them through non-sexual touches and kissing hello or goodbye, sitting together or snuggling, holding hands and verbalizing affection or what you find sexy about your spouse.

A recent example of this is with our marriage check-up we did.

I explained to Marcus that although I love making love with him, I felt like it was lacking in some areas. We are very open with our communication about everything including sex, but I still didn't want him to feel like he was inadequate. I didn't want him to feel bad. I explained we needed more foreplay and more nights where we just made out like back when we were dating. I needed more flirting throughout the day, more touching, even non-sexual touches.

He listened, asked a few questions about what I meant exactly and in the month that followed things have gotten better than ever. Because I was willing to communicate my needs to him, even though it was a little uncomfortable, our sex life and marriage have gotten that much better. We grew closer and continue trying to improve our marriage. – Ashley

The more you talk about your sex life with your spouse, the easier it gets. Your spouse cannot read your mind and if you feel like they are missing the spot (both literally and figuratively) then tell them…or show them! If you want to have sex, communicate it to your spouse and ask for an answer. That way your spouse knows that you want to make love and they can mentally or physically prepare. If your spouse is not ready to have sex, they can communicate that to you so you don't get too worked up over feeling rejected or frustrated when you are expecting to be intimate and it does not happen.

Did you know that you and your spouse will probably have different expectations about sex in marriage? Did you know your expectation of how often you want to have sex will change in the different seasons of life? Communicate to our spouse how often you would like to make love, see how often they want to, and compromise on a frequency. Just as you have expectations of how often you will make love, you have expectations of the kind of sex you want to have. Again, this will change throughout your life or the day of the week. So you need to remember to communicate to your spouse as your sexual expectations evolve.

Ask your spouse how many times a week they want to make love. How many times do you want to? Then find a number you can both agree on. In our marriage, one of us wants to make love about five times a week and the other is quite happy with twice. We had to talk about this and decide on a minimum number that we could compromise on. We decided three times a week with flexibility for spontaneity fit our situation. This may not be a challenge for some newlyweds. As your marriage progresses and children possibly come along, you should keep this bit of advice filed away. It helps open the line of communication about your sexual relationship, which will be richer for it.

Some couples schedule sex down to which days of the week one will initiate and which days another will. While other couples have found that having a minimum number of times a week they can expect to be able to connect sexually with their spouse is comforting. Mixing up how you take turns initiating sex as well as where and when you have sex can keep the spice in your marriage.

Flirt, flirt, and keep flirting like you did when you were dating! Flirting in whichever way your spouse receives it best will help you to keep the fire burning. Prepare your mind, romance and connect with your spouse from the time you wake up in the morning. You can't expect to ignore your spouse all day and expect him or her to be ready to make love after the kids go to bed. Connection needs to happen throughout the day. While physical and direct sexual touches works for some, it can be a turn off for others. So ask your spouse when and how they feel wanted and turned on. The way both you and your spouse feel romanced is different. It will change over the different periods and different days in your life.

Communicating what you like is the first step to receiving what you want in and out of the bedroom. Keeping the conversation open about your sexual relationship will help enrich variety, deeper understanding, and a better sex life. It can be hard sometimes. We have felt the frustration of trying to communicate something to our spouse and they are just not getting it. This is where we try to change the way we explain it to them. Instead of words, show them physically. Have fun with it, sex is supposed to be an enjoyable experience by all.

Sex is one of the most important aspects of your marriage. Sexual intimacy is the way you and your spouse get to connect and become one in a way you don't with anyone else. So keep sex a priority in your marriage. The physical connection is an intimate expression of the special love you both share with each other. Sex is also a great stress reliever.

When we had our first daughter it was difficult at first for me to switch mindsets; from mommy mode to wife mode. It was not easy. I wanted to hold, and nurture this tiny human that grew inside of me, but also be intimate with Marcus. I wanted to able to focus on that physical connection with my husband without constantly wanting to check on our newborn baby.

One way I did this was to prepare my mind ahead of time. I did this by listening to romantic music, thinking about my husband and everything I love about him. – Ashley

Once you become parents, you may find a new fondness for quickies. It is essential you make sure you are connecting physically when you are ready and sometimes quickies are the answer. Just be sure that you both are feeling like your needs are being met sexually. That can be a big adjustment after a baby!

Whether you become a parent or not, your sex life will not be stationary. You will go through changes throughout your marriage, just make sure that the communication channel is open and honest.

Sometimes marriages can go through a dry spell. It is essential to keep your sex life active and keep you both connected in that physical way. Try spicing things up. Keep trying new things and add variety to your sex life. Try new positions, make love in different rooms or places, share fantasies, have a lot of foreplay can help spice things up. Give your spouse feedback about what you like, what doesn't work, how and where you want them to touch you. Recreating the time you made love for the first time together can also be a fun way to remember together. Remember to take care of your body and keep good hygiene.

You should both be trying to learn each other's bodies and the spots that give your spouse ultimate pleasure. You do this through experimenting, variety, trying new things, and communicating to each other. You have to talk or show each other because your spouse cannot read your mind. If you do not ask, you probably will not receive. Throughout your marriage, you will try new and different sexual things with your spouse in your bedroom. You will go from, "I will never do that" to, "Wow, it feels great. Let's do it again."

One very important note to make is that your sex life details should be between the two of you. This does not mean you can't ask for advice and tips, or ideas to spice things up from friends or family members. Just remember that sex is an intimate experience. If you share the details of that experience, it isn't so exclusive anymore is it? You might also embarrass or disrespect your spouse, so talk to them and ask them what they are comfortable with you sharing. A good rule of thumb is if you are not comfortable saying it to people in front of your spouse then don't say it at all.

You probably have heard this statement before: "What happens in the bedroom stays in the bedroom." It is so true when it comes to marriage. The moment you share your bedroom secrets with friends, parents, relatives, etc., you have broken the trust you have with your spouse. As you know, when trust is broken, it is *very* difficult to rebuild. It could take months, years, or even decades to restore it.

When you reveal your bedroom secrets to other people, it negatively impacts every aspect of the marriage. Sex becomes a chore instead of a gift, and intimacy vanishes into thin air. The trust your spouse has for you should never be taken for granted. During our first year, we had no kids. Our sex life was amazing. We made love a lot. Then the kids came and our sex life had to change.

After having our first child, Ashley's body went through a lot of changes, from physical to emotional to sexual changes. She was not interested in sex like I was; which was surprising. However after talking about the change in her sexual drive, she was able to explain things to me in a better way.

I also did some research to learn more about the changes women go through after having a baby. For instance, I learned new things like understanding the hormonal changes happening to her body, reasons why she felt touched out and tired on some days, etc. In fact, my research was key to us bringing back the spark to our sexual intimacy. I was well informed which helped me to better understand and connect with her intimately.

As a husband, I now encourage other husbands to take a few minutes to research on reasons why their wives might be acting in a certain way. It definitely helps to get a better picture of the situation. – Marcus

Your sex life will impact your marriage in many ways so invest in learning more about how the body of your spouse works. Have open discussions about sex and explore your bodies with each other and work through any insecurities you may have to better your sexual relationship.

We have listed some great questions in chapter eleven to help you both to better understand each other's sexual expectations and desires.

Sex is an emotion in motion.

– Mae West

Spirituality

Spirituality is such an integral part of our life on earth whether you believe in a God, gods, goddess, or no higher power at all. To think it should be kept separate from marriage would be like thinking you can hide a part of yourself.

We began our marriage having the same faith. In fact, it was a deal-breaker for Marcus that whoever he decided to marry had to also believe in the same core belief system. As we progressed through our marriage and life together, we realized we were coming to a crossroads.

When we were first married we both identified as Christians. We both explained that sharing the same religion was important to us and to help make marriage work, because that is what we had been taught. Since then I have began searching for answers to questions about Christianity I have had for a long time and never got any real answers to. I shared my concerns with Marcus from the beginning. We talked about them. I listened to his advice and consulted with certain people he suggested. I began a soul searching and fact-checking journey that has still not ended.

I remember being in the kitchen with our girls eating dinner as I was sharing the latest information I had learned about the growing questions and doubt I had. I told Marcus I didn't believe in the fundamental beliefs of Christianity anymore; that I didn't believe in Jesus or anything I have been raised to believe all my life. Even though I had kept him in the loop with everything along my journey and discoveries, this came as a shock to him. Marcus didn't completely understand me. He made a comment about not being able to be together anymore. I asked him to repeat what he just said to make sure I heard him right.

I tried to stay calm as my heart started to break. I took our baby in the bedroom to get ready for bath. But really, it was to process things and not show my toddler I was upset. I loved this man with all my heart and wanted to be with him, but I couldn't lie to him or myself. Putting on an act was not an option. I had done enough acting in my life.

After a few minutes he came into the bedroom and saw my tears. We talked and he had assumed that meant I was going to join other religious groups and become confrontational. I explained that was not the case at all. I simply have lost my belief in Christianity and everything I had been taught was truth. I had begun questioning things long ago and he knew that. I told him I still believed in a Higher Power. I wasn't joining another religious group. I had had enough religion to last me a lifetime. That presented him with a major relief.

This was his deal-breaker, but he molded it because we were changing. He apologized and said he wanted to stay married to me and assured me he loved me. That was one of the scariest conversations in our marriage. Honestly, I was a little gun shy after that. – Ashley

Our point in sharing this story is so that you can see how much molding, changing, and compromising goes on in a marriage. The person you married will change over time. We should be open-minded and try our hardest to make things work with each other. However, it is also healthy to have boundaries.

I was hurt when Ashley told me she no longer believed in Christ. Having the same belief was very important for me, especially in how we raised our kids so hearing those words from Ashley was not easy.

I felt disappointed and thought that was the end of our marriage. Could we be getting divorced? Is this the end of our marriage after everything we had been through? How will this

impact our marriage? Can a couple have a fulfilling marriage even though they are not of the same faith?

I pondered over these questions a lot. I came to the conclusion that yes, she does not believe in Christ, but that does not mean we should get divorced. It does not mean we cannot have a fulfilling marriage because I have seen couples of the same faith getting divorced and vice versa. The good thing was that because we communicate frequently about our feelings, what we are going through as individuals, discovering and learning more about ourselves, Ashley had informed me about her quest to find what she believes in through previous conversations. She had a lot of questions about her faith, did her own research and came to a conclusion. She believes there is a Higher Power and to her, the same Higher Power has a different name for different people.

I personally believe that she made a good decision for herself instead of lying to herself to believe in my faith just to make me happy. – Marcus

We truly and honestly believe that if two people can have an open mind and be respectful of each other's beliefs then you can each believe totally opposite religions or personal belief systems. We agreed to not raise our children with any religion or dogma. So, as they grow they can ask questions and do their own research on the personal journey of spirituality. That way their beliefs are their own and not something they believe because they were told to, or out of fear of hypothetical consequences.

If you and your spouse can share whatever commonalities your beliefs have together, it can help you grow closer and appreciate your differences more. If you sit and meditate together, share the character lessons you are learning, or whatever you can find to do together on a spiritual level, it will improve your marriage.

Marriage should be about love, acceptance for each individuality, respect, and growth. Why shouldn't this be included in our spiritual aspect of life? For a marriage to last and be fulfilling both individuals need to work towards creating the marriage they both desire. Whether you and your spouse are of the same faith or not, it is the marriage skills, dedication, commitment, respect, and love for each other that will impact your marriage the most. There will come a time that believing in yourself is not going to be enough. You both have to believe in something bigger than yourself.

Chapter 7

Setting Boundaries

Boundaries represent awareness, knowing what the limits are and then respecting those limits.

– David W. Earle

Setting boundaries is one of the most important things you need to do at the beginning of your marriage. As newlyweds, it can be hard to figure out how you and your spouse function as a unit separate from the family dynamics you have known all your life. You have to create your new normal. For us, those boundaries were being set up beginning with the wedding planning.

We decided on having a small wedding with just a few friends and family that lived nearby. We had a very small budget to work with and wanted to keep it simple. Our families offered helpful ideas that were not always well received.

The one thing that sticks out in my memory is my mother wanted us to have giant hula-hoops for everyone to use. Some of my relatives also wanted to do a dance to techno music. I was horrified by the thought of meeting my husband–to–be's extended family and them getting the wrong impression of my family.

We are from two different cultures, and their wedding ceremonies are big and taken very seriously (from my limited experience). Looking back I can see how this seemed like such a huge deal back then; now we laugh about it. Anyways, we had to stand united and let them know that the hula-hoops and techno noise (I mean, music) wouldn't be tolerated. These events wouldn't mesh well with the theme for our wedding. – Ashley

The above example is one of the ways we used to start creating boundaries for our marriage and the new family unit we were about to create. It is hard and very awkward at first if you are not used to setting boundaries as an individual. We recommend reading the books *Boundaries* and *Boundaries in Marriage*, both are written by Dr. Henry Cloud.

In the beginning, you might find it hard not feeling guilty, or like you *should* be doing something because they are your parents/in-laws. Another challenge is recognizing someone who is manipulative. Recognizing these characteristics in the way someone speaks, acts, or the words they use helps a lot. Watch out for phrases people use for manipulation, like, "If you loved me…", "but we're family…", "I have no one else…", "You should…", "Is that the right thing to do/not do…", "You never…", "You always…", etc. Set firm boundaries with anyone who tries to guilt and manipulate you into doing something. If you have to distance yourself from them, do it. It will help your marriage.

Boundaries need to be created within your extended family, immediate family, in-laws, friends, co-workers, and other relationships in general. Healthy boundaries will help you grow together in your marriage with less resistance from outside your boundary zone. Staying united about which boundaries you choose and enforcing them is the first and most important step to take.

37 Questions for Creating Boundaries

Ask each other these questions to help you discover which boundaries you want to create:

Marriage

» What if you find yourself attracted to another person and entertaining thoughts of cheating?

» What do you both define as cheating?

» What is not okay in your marriage (Deal breakers)?

» You have to respect and accept that your spouse is a different human being than yourself.

» How do you feel about close friends who you talk to or spend more time with than your spouse?

Family

» Have you talked about what kind of boundaries you want to set with your families?

» What will you do when your family pressures you to have children before you are ready?

» What will you do when family pressures you to buy a house before you are financially ready?

» How often will family members visit?

» How often will you visit them?

» What times are good for phone calls and visits?

» Which holidays will be celebrated where?

» How much money will you spend on gifts?

» Can family or friends borrow money from you?

» Who is the one to talk to which family members about these boundaries needing to be enforced?

» What things are private and should be kept between just you and your spouse? Things like your sex life, or your money? *Abuse and addiction should never be kept private and you should seek help immediately. *

Parenting

» Children throw a whole new mix into setting boundaries with relatives.

» Who can be around your child?

» What will you do if your relatives or friends do not respect your dietary wishes for your child?

» What will you do if your discipline/teaching wishes are not respected?

» Who can discipline your child and how?

» Who cannot be alone with your child?

Friendships

» What about boundaries with friendships?

» What will you do if a friend makes a pass at you?

» What are topics that should not be shared with anyone like details your sexual relationship, money, etc.

» Is it okay to be alone with certain friends?

» Is it okay to loan friends money?

» Is it okay to borrow from friends?

» Can your friends call and visit at any time?

» How often will you have a girls/guys night?

Work relationships

- » Is there anyone not okay to be alone with?
- » What will you do if a co-worker makes a pass at you?
- » Which topics are not open to discussion with co-workers?
- » Which days do you absolutely have to have off?
- » What if something happens and one of you or your children is ill?
- » How much over time is too much over time?

You get the idea? There are so many questions or issues that you probably haven't thought about needing to discuss, but now you do. More than once, because your opinions on these matters will probably change as you both grow. You need to realize how you feel about these questions and how you want things to go. Unless you ask your spouse how they would answer these questions, you really don't know what their answer will be. It might surprise you. Spend some time with your spouse to talk about the boundaries you need to set for your marriage and your life. It will help you both to avoid unnecessary arguments married couples; especially newlyweds, have in the first year. You will both know what to expect and it will guide your transition into married life.

When it comes to setting boundaries for communicating with your in-laws, there is a simple and proven way of communicating with in-laws that has worked very well for us as well as other married couples. It's this: whenever you need to convey a message to your in-laws, let your spouse be the one to tell them. Your spouse knows and understands your in-laws better than you do. So why not let them do the talking on your behalf. When you present your decision to them it means you and your spouse have already had the chance to discuss things and come to an agreement. That way you have a united front. Never feel obliged to fulfill expectations your family members have for your marriage, instead focus on creating the kind of marriage you both want.

Families living in dysfunction seldom have healthy boundaries. Dysfunctional families have trouble knowing where they stop and others begin.

– David W. Earle

Another way of looking at it is to imagine you and your parents speak English while your spouse and their parents speak French. Who will be the best person in your marriage to communicate with each other's in-laws? This is especially important when communicating about your decision to wait to buy a house or have children until you are ready.

Discussing the boundaries for your marriage is not a one-time conversation. Just as all things in marriage, it is continuous.

Life is unpredictable, things change, views change, and situations change. So talk about your boundaries again every so often when you think your views are changing or just feel like it is time for a check in. What is right for you now, may not be right for you in a year. Be open. Be honest. Communicate your thoughts to your spouse. You both want to be together and create a life together. You are both on the same team. Make sure you are working towards the same goals.

Having a mentor for your marriage can help you recognize other areas of your relationship that needs improvement as well as holding you accountable. We love to find couples that have been married for longer periods of time and are still very much in love with a strong friendship. These individuals may not even know what to tell you, but by being with them and observing how they interact, they will unconsciously show you.

If you are honestly in a position that there are no other couples around you that you feel you could look up to and learn from, check out the wealth of information through books, podcasts, YouTube videos, and seminars. Examples of podcasts are the *First Year Marriage Show* and *One Extraordinary Marriage Show* podcasts on iTunes. We have also created a list of awesome podcasts, which can be found by visiting www.ourpeacefulfamily.com/marriagepodcasts.

One of the neat things about starting your own family unit by getting married is the ability to create your own traditions. Just because you have always done things or celebrated a holiday the same way, doesn't mean you have to forever. Being married you have to mix your cultures and traditions as well as create your own. Keep what you love, lose what you don't. We have done this by celebrating Christmas on Christmas Eve and staying home on Christmas or going to the park or sledding with our kids. Creating our own meaning for the holidays, especially after learning the true history and meanings of holidays that our history books didn't tell us.

Our traditions are always evolving too. We just decided this year that we would no longer do a traditional birthday party every year with friends. Instead, we will do a small party with family and maybe one friend. Then we put all the money we would have put towards a party and use it to go somewhere and make it about the experience.

These changes in tradition are not always welcomed by your families, but change can be scary for many people.

Remember when you get married you are leaving your parents and join together with your spouse. This doesn't mean you forget you have a family and they are no longer a priority. This just means they are moving down the priority list a little bit. Your spouse comes before your family in a healthy relationship. You want to be sure to try to include those close to you, but also do what you both feel is right. Setting boundaries in the areas of traditions can be tricky, but not impossible. It helps if you do it one step at a time, clearly communicating your reason *why* this change is so important to you.

Chapter 8
Nurturing Your Marriage

A dream you dream alone is only a dream. A dream you dream together is reality.

– John Lennon

Connecting and growing together as a couple is so vital to nurturing your marriage. When you are first married it may seem easy, but life and kids can make connecting and growing together become more of a challenge. You have to purpose each day to connect with your spouse for at least an hour. We do this in the evening after our kids go to sleep. We love this time of connecting with each other. We can laugh, reminisce, and plan ahead for our future. We share with each other what we are learning, how we are growing, and what we have been feeling.

In the beginning of your relationship, you spent time getting to know each other. You were opening up and sharing your feelings, fears, joys, and dreams together. You were curious about your spouse. Never let that curiosity and motivation to know your spouse fade away. Continue pursuing and learning more about each other. If you do, you will not simply exist together in 5, 10, 20, or 70 years' time; you will connect, grow together, and never feel like strangers.

After many couples get married, they forget to keep dating their spouse or they get busy. It is easy to have the fantasy that you know everything there is to know about your spouse, but the reality is we are always growing and changing so no matter how many years you are married there is always something new to learn about your spouse. New interests, new projects, new dreams, or plans. So connecting with your spouse through dates helps cultivate your friendship, your romance, and even aids you in learning more about your spouse.

12 Simple Ways to Connect and Grow With Your Spouse

1. A conversation.

Not just about the daily stuff, but about the two of you. A dialogue about your marriage and what you are learning or excited about. These conversations should be at least an hour. Why? Because sometimes it takes a little while to get into a deep or meaningful discussion that makes you feel connected. Make sure your phones and other technology is not a distraction.

2. Dream together.

Look forward to something together. Make some plans, no matter how far into the future. Plan vacations, travel plans, building a house, moving, starting a business, anything that gets you both excited for something. Dreaming together is one of our favorite things to do when we have our conversations.

3. Play a game or do something fun together.

Laughing together will help you both to bond together, release stress, and keep you focused on having fun as a couple.

4. Touch!

Hold hands while you talk, or snuggle under a blanket together on the couch. Get the oxytocin flowing!

5. Get outside your comfort zone.

Do something that gets you both a little outside of your comfort zone and try something new. It can be an activity, cuisine, or whatever you can come up with as long as it is different! We tried learning tennis together this year and had a blast while getting a work out.

6. Set goals together.

Set goals for your marriage, family, life, careers, etc. Goals are so important for a marriage to thrive. Because by voicing these goals, it ensures you both know what you are working towards so you are continually growing and working together. Remember to write them down.

7. Read at least one book together every year.

We like to choose marriage, relational or books on honing character qualities that are beneficial to our marriage. That way we can have discussions about the books and what we learned.

8. Check in during the day.

Shoot your spouse a text, e-mail, or call them to see how their day is going. It lets them know you are thinking about them.

9. Date your spouse.

Whether you want to make this a weekly, bi-weekly, or monthly event is up to you and your schedule. Take some time for just the two of you. Even if that means you wait until the kids are asleep and you stay in. Use that time to connect, talk and laugh. It is important to be able to get away from the kids and be just the two of you whenever that is possible.

10. Eat together.

Cooking is always a fun time for us since we both love cooking whole healthy foods. Cooking together with some music on and eating your dinner together every night is a great way to wind down after a long day. Breakfast together is a great way to connect and start your day. Do whatever works with your schedule.

11. Work side by side.

We enjoy working on our own individual projects in the same room together when our girls are asleep. Try building something together, gardening together, or sitting next to each other while you do some needed reading with your bodies close. Marcus loves side-by-side interaction. When you see men talking they generally don't always try to keep eye contact whereas women tend to like more face-to-face interaction.

12. Being still together.

Connecting with your spouse doesn't always have to involve talking and doing an activity. Sometimes just laying or sitting next to your spouse snuggling can be an awesome way to connect. It is even more fun if you are naked.

In the beginning of our marriage, we had very busy schedules, so we set aside, at the very least, 10 – 15 minutes to connect every day. We now know the importance of carving out at least 1-hour every night, even more on the weekends, to spend connecting with each other in these different ways. Our marriage has grown so much because of it. It relieves stress, brings us closer, and helps us appreciate each other more. Our friendship is flourishing because we are intentionally cultivating it. Trust us, your marriage will benefit by spending time together every day connecting.

As humans we are always learning and growing, or at least we should be. When we get married it can be easy for some to think that you are not an individual any longer. Terms such as *two become one* can help muddle that confusion. However, remember you are and always will be an individual. When you decide to get married and commit to spend your life with another person, you are simply saying that you will put their needs and happiness as a priority for yourself and not just think about your own. Your wife wants to feel secure and loved. Your husband wants to feel appreciated and respected.

You became a team by deciding to get married. Your *I* becomes *We*, and *Me* becomes *Us*. Now you must think about what is best for the team with the individual goals you brought together, and continue to work on as a team. There must still be a balance where you can grow as an individual and have some *me* time.

You both must be growing as individuals and together as a couple. You don't want to be growing and changing and not let your spouse know everything that is happening with you. This is one way couples grow apart. On the other end of the spectrum, you don't want to not be growing and enhancing your life because you may fall behind while your spouse is progressing.

We had a conversation the other day about how different we are today, than when we first got married. We have changed quite a bit, thankfully our character qualities have evolved, as well as our beliefs about so many things. We always purpose to grow as individuals and as a couple. We love to learn and inquire about things we don't understand. After having kids, our interests have changed and continue to do so as we learn new things about ourselves, kids, marriage, and parenting. It is all about balancing and finding out what your marriage needs and when it needs it. The only way to do that is to learn how to communicate with your spouse and find out what's going on with them.

Learn how your spouse gives and receives love in the most effective way. To keep that in love feeling takes work as your love matures into the greatest and most intimate relationship you will have with another person on this earth. Learn how to love your spouse by learning how they receive love the best by checking out The Five Love Languages by Gary Chapman. You can take the free quiz online, which can be found here: www.5lovelanguages.com/profile.

You do not want to wake up years from today only to find you have grown apart and have nothing in common. Look for activities that you both enjoy and do them together. This simple tip can help you grow together and improve your intimacy. Make connecting and growing together a daily habit even if you both have extremely busy careers, responsibilities, etc.

Connecting with your spouse on a regular basis will set your marriage foundation up for success.

The Gift of Friendship

Coming together is a beginning; keeping together is progress; working together is success.

– Henry Ford

Friendship is the lifeblood of a marriage. Your spouse should become your best friend. You have to cultivate that friendship by connecting and spending time together doing different activities. Growing your friendship will help your marriage flourish in all areas. Your sex life will get better, your stress will be better managed, and your happiness will increase. How do you grow your friendship with your spouse? By connecting and purposefully making your marriage your top priority. Carve out time and schedule it so it happens! We know life gets busy, especially when kids are thrown into the mix, so be intentional.

Your spouse has committed to spending their life with you. So why not choose them to be your best friend? Having your spouse as your best friend is certainly one of the best perks for marriage. We have enjoyed being best friends and look forward to the growing together in the years to come.

I remember when we were dating and Marcus had a friend who is like a brother to him. I referred to his friend as his best friend. Marcus corrected me and said that was a title he was saving for his wife. Obviously I became his best friend, and that is something special between us. – Ashley

Ever since the time I knew I wanted to have a family some-day, I came to the conclusion that the person I settle down with will become my best friend.

This is a decision I made and a title I reserved just for her. – Marcus

Never discount the essence of having close friends simply because your spouse is your best friend. Your close friends should be the ones to quickly identify, and recommend changes in certain behaviors you and your spouse may never notice. They should also challenge you to love your spouse and improve your marriage.

Friendship in marriage builds intimacy and helps married couples to open up to their insecurities without worrying about being judged. The term *falling out of love* comes to mind. If you nourish your friendship with your spouse as well as your intimacy, your marriage should blossom into a beautiful friendship with a deep mature love. We have experienced this in our marriage.

Taking time to celebrate all your accomplishments together as a couple is a good way to share the small (or big) accomplishments of your life together. Make sure you celebrate all the goals you achieve as well as your first anniversary together (and all the anniversaries to come!).

Think about all the attributes you want in a best friend and write them down. Ask your spouse what they also want in a best friend. Then work hard on yourself to become the best friend you want to see in your spouse as well as what they need from friendship. Your marriage will be taken to another level.

7 Tips to Becoming Best Friends

The action steps below will help you and your spouse on your journey to becoming best friends. Practice them every day and you will become best friends as your marriage grows.

1. Be there to cheer each other on.

2. Grow together. Hand in hand partnership and participate in activities together.

3. Connect with each other in different ways.

4. Be there for your spouse to lean on you during the tough times your spouse and your marriage goes through.

5. Be honest and sincere, so you and your spouse can trust each other.

6. Share in the joys, victories, achievements, and successes of each other.

7. Appreciate each other.

Laugh together! Fun should be a part of your marriage. When we are laughing together or having fun together, it helps remind us of why we fell in love with this person, why we chose to spend every day for the remainder of this life together. It is so easy to get caught up in the busyness of life and seriousness of it all. Laughing with your spouse will help you relieve stress, grow closer and enjoy your time together. Nurturing friendship in marriage requires practice and intentionality. If you are not intentional about it, it will not just show up. Just like any friendship and relationship it takes nourishment to grow. It requires time and effort.

Physical things don't last. The physical will fade away, but true friendship will last. True emotional and spiritual intimacy in friendship transcends time. Friendship is one of the many characteristics of a healthy, happy, and lasting marriage. Not to mention one of the best parts of your spouse being your best friend is you get to share a bed.

A Weekly Marriage Checkup

Having a marriage check-up is a great way for maintaining a healthy marriage. Marriage check-up is a great way to learn how to communicate with your spouse. Setting up a time that you set aside to connect and talk with your spouse about the temperature of your marriage, discussing any progress or retrogression made, and the goals you set for your marriage is very important.

We do a weekly marriage check-up. Some of the questions we always ask each other during our check-ups are, "Are you happy in all areas of our marriage? Social, sexual, friendship, daily life, fun aspect, etc." We also ask each other, "Give me something I can work on to improve about myself that will better me and our marriage."

Communicating with each other is something we all have to continue learning and practicing. Marriage check-ups presents us with an opportunity to do just that. You have to be open and honest with each other. You have to be willing to listen to your spouse, be open-minded to accept critique and know that your spouse has the best intentions for you. It might be challenging at first to not take things as a direct insult. Instead, view them as a form of constructive critique.

Learning how to approach topics with your spouse is part of the journey on communicating with your spouse. Our marriage check-ups go a whole lot smoother than our earlier ones. We actually have fewer critiques for each other as we continue to grow together and improve ourselves. This will be the same for every married couple, because we are all unique, but every couple should have a marriage check-up.

We read a story from a woman who asked her husband not just, "Are you happy with our relationship?" and "Is there anywhere I can improve for our family and marriage?" She asked where her husband thought she was in her potential on a scale of 1 to 10. Ten being the best wife, mother, and person she could be.

We can see how this could get heated if you are too insecure to be able to accept a healthy critique. It is something we learn and grow through. If your spouse is a respectful, loving individual and you have a healthy marriage, it should be a safe place to talk about this stuff to help you grow as a person and as a couple.

10 Benefits of Marriage Check-ups

1. It brings you closer together as a couple in more ways than one, discovering more about each other.

2. Teaches you how to better communicate with each other.

3. Helps you work through insecurities, learning your strengths and weaknesses.

4. Encourages honesty in your marriage.

5. Gives you a safe and open space to both give and receive critiques to help you grow as an individual.

6. Personal growth helps your marriage progress, while helping you to grow together with your spouse.

7. Creates happiness when both spouses feel they are heard and see each other making efforts to create a better life.

8. Keeps you on track with your marriage, family, and life goals.

9. Holds each other accountable. Who better to do this than the person who knows you the best and your partner in life?

10. Helps to identify issues before they turn into major marriage problems.

How to Have Your Marriage Check-up

First, discuss its importance and the benefits with your spouse so you can both agree to do it regularly. Let your spouse know why you want one and the important role your spouse will play in your marriage check-up.

Set a regular time (weekly, monthly, bi-monthly) that you can both sit down and have this check-up. *The check-up should not be taken for granted.*

Ask each other this question: "Tell me one thing you think I can improve on so I can continue to become better for myself, our family, and marriage."

Lastly, be honest and go to work on improving your marriage, family, and life.

One thing you should ask each other every week is: on a scale of 1 to 10, how would you rate our marriage relationship this week? How would you rate our sex life this week? How would you rate our connection this week? Anything less than 10 should have a reason, so talk about it and see what you can do to improve in the following week.

In a healthy marriage with respect and love, your spouse is your best friend. The one you can talk about anything and everything with. He or she is your safe person and should be honest with you for the good of your marriage. Your spouse should know you better than anyone else. You live with him/her under the same roof, share the same bed, share the good times, as well as the bad times with. Your spouse sees you at your best and your worst; which makes it that much more important to be on the same page and make sure you are both feeling happy, connected, fulfilled, and content in all areas of your marriage.

By having a check-up with your spouse, you will be on the same page or at least know where you both are in terms of your finances, emotions, spiritual growth, physical, and intellectual state.

Great things are done by a series of small things brought together.

– Vincent Van Gogh

Chapter 9

In Sickness and Health, for Richer, for Poorer

Sometimes our light goes out, but is blown again into instant flame by an encounter with another human being.

– Albert Schweitzer

When most people get married and picture their life they expect a happily ever after. Is it wishful thinking or a Disney character naivety? These struggles, which are a part of life, are what can tear marriages apart. You have to prepare for them as much as you can and be ready to stick together through the ups and the downs of life.

Having a partner to go through this roller coaster of life can be one of the best parts of marriage.

I can honestly say that I did not expect us to struggle financially as much as we did. Because of Marcus' visa work restrictions we drained the little savings we had for lawyers. I did odd jobs whenever I could, but I was definitely feeling the stress.

I worked three different part time jobs while going to school full time. Student loan debt was racking up. We didn't have much to spend on food so fruit was a novelty. We finally broke down and went to a food shelf for some food and help with paying two months of rent. We were so lucky to have two amazing landlords who gave us a huge deal on rent, we did not want to take advantage of their kindness.

This lack of money caused a huge stress on me. When I looked at the budget and saw the amount needed and then the fact there was no money to pay any of those bills while I was exhausted from doing everything I could to make that money was frustrating to say the least. Marcus saw this and he took over paying the bills and doing most of the finances; we still budgeted together. We just kept our head down and took it one day one moment at a time.

Then we found out I was pregnant. Surprise! At this point Marcus was not allowed to work and I had switched to online classes so I could work more hours. We were excited and scared. We went to the doctor's office and he told me I was high risk for a miscarriage because I had an IUD. It was a terrifying thing to hear (and a risk I specifically asked the doctor who inserted it, she assured me it was not). Thankfully we did not lose our baby.

Once Marcus was able to work, he got a job. We saved every extra penny we could in case we ever got in the situation again. We built our emergency fund up again…then he was laid off from work for a few months. Our emergency fund held over just in time for taxes to come in. We lived off that until Marcus was called back to work.

Eventually he went back to school to finish his college degree so he could get a better job. I had our first daughter and stayed home with her while he worked and went to school while running an online business he started. The man had no free time.

After nearly four years of no money and struggling to get through school with more times of job loss and layoff, we made it. He graduated and we moved out of the country to the city here in Vermont (which is very suburban). Marcus got a great job and we spent a year and all our tax refund money catching up. We spent a great summer together and then I was diagnosed with an autoimmune disease.

I was diagnosed with Hashimotos thyroiditis. This means my own immune system is attacking parts of my body. I had to change my lifestyle drastically through diet, supplements, stress levels and limit my activity. This put strain on us financially once again as well as affecting our daily life. It was good to have the diagnoses so we could understand why I was so forgetful and had such fatigue. It helped Marcus understand and have more patience when I forgot what I was saying or complete conversations we had.

This also meant that our children will be more susceptible to allergies and autoimmune diseases. We prepare and try to prevent that through living a clean lifestyle free of harsh chemicals, genetically modified foods, fresh and local produce, and meats treated without hormones and antibiotics.

Reducing stress and pacing our daily life has played a large role as well. We are working together to get this into remission, because there is no cure. –Ashley

Communication has been so important throughout our marriage, especially in these challenges we face. We understand how losing a job and career stress can wreak havoc on a marriage. It is easy to lose motivation and feel sorry for yourself or like you are not good enough. The truth is, you have to keep going taking it day by day, hand in hand because you are in this together. During a job loss it is imperative that you communicate your feelings and struggles with each other.

If Marcus hadn't communicated to me that he felt like a failure, I might not have been so sensitive to his feelings and he would have felt alone. It could have torn us apart. – Ashley

If Ashley hadn't communicated that she was okay with everything she had to do, and that I would get to do this again, I would have felt defeated and alone. If she hadn't expressed her stress over the finances, I wouldn't have known to take over to help relieve her of that. – Marcus

Because we were willing to be open with each other, even though it was hard opening up about these feelings, our marriage would have imploded. Effort from both spouses is so vital when dealing with these struggles.

When we discovered I could not work to help support us I had a hard time accepting that. I felt like a parasite. Like I was a failure as a man because a man is supposed to provide for his family. It made me appreciate the fact that you can lose something you have (my ability to work) and it doesn't mean it's the end of your life. You can use that as an opportunity to better your life and yourself.

Ashley told me it wasn't my fault and that I shouldn't feel like I wasn't providing. At that point she was the one who needed to work and provide and there would come a time when I would be able to do that for her. That made me feel at ease that she understood I wasn't being lazy and that she wasn't blaming me.

While I could not work due to my visa situation, I spent most of my time reading books like Entreleadership by Dave Ramsey, 100 Dollar Start Up by Chris Guillebeau, My Philosophy for Successful Living by Jim Rohn, etc. In addition, I did all the house chores, cooking, and everything in-between to make things easier for Ashley. The books I read inspired me to start an online business while I was in college, which led to us blogging about our first year of marriage, hosting the First Year Marriage Show podcast and now writing books to share our marriage experience and the lessons we have learned to help other couples.

Learning your spouse has an autoimmune disease that is not curable, is scary. In fact, the side effects of the disease, financial impact on your budget and life changes alone could easily stress you out. After learning about Ashley's autoimmune disease, I spent time learning a bit about it. I prepared myself to be able to support her as she goes through these changes. To be honest, it was not easy for me in the beginning as it made our budget tighter than we expected.

We keep our communication open about the changes she is going through, the different diet changes, basically keeping me in the loop so if I need to help or do more research I can do that. She lets me know when she needs more help or more rest. We talk about how I feel and how I am coping too because we are in this together. – Marcus

Because you are both committed to helping each other through the ups and downs, use this as an opportunity to improve your marriage and intimacy. If you are the one experiencing the health issues, you need your spouse's support, and vice versa. We have learned and grown so much through these hard times. We used all the tools we talk about in this book to get through these times of hardship in our marriage. That is why it is so important to share our journey with you, because we know just how important each of these skills are.

Ask yourself and your spouse how you believe you would react to these situations:

» A job loss.

» A miscarriage.

» Breach of trust.

» Depression.

» Anxiety struggles.

» Finding out one of you has a health issue.

» Surprise pregnancy.

» Finding out a child has an illness or other learning challenges.

» Death of a loved one.

Communicating effectively throughout your marriage is so integral to the very fiber of your union; it is that much more imperative when going through challenging times. There is a good chance your spouse will have no idea what you are going through and not know how to deal with it at first. Patience while learning what you can to help each other can go a long way.

I was so frustrated that Ashley was forgetting so much. I was really irritated when I would ask her to do something, or we would talk about something, and she would completely forget soon after.

Receiving Ashley's diagnoses of Hashimotos helped me to be able to understand why this was going on and enables me to be more patient with her and prepared for the forgetfulness. She even uses a white board in the kitchen to help her remember and I help her too. – Marcus

There is always a reason to why your spouse is acting the way they are. It may not be an autoimmune disease, but it could be stress, being too busy, anxiety, depression, etc. Maybe you can help your spouse realize they are under too much stress or taking on too many activities. Help each other to balance your life and be empathetic.

We know you may not go through the same struggles as we did, but you will go through some sort of conflict as some point. Financial stress, job loss, infertility, death of a loved one, loss of trust, health issues the list of possibilities is endless. It makes no sense in dwelling on what *could happen,* but you need to prepare your marriage for the storms that may come by building a strong foundation. Build and maintain that foundation for the success of a healthy and fulfilling marriage. That is why we wrote this book. We wholeheartedly believe that a strong foundation in these key areas we talked about in this book will help you stand the tests of time as long as you intentionally cultivate.

Chapter 10

How to Create a Vision for Your Marriage and Family

The only thing worse than being blind is having sight but no vision.

– Helen Keller

O ne thing that will help you and your spouse get on the same page on how you grow and connect together as a new family unit is to choose a theme for your marriage and family. Choosing a theme for your family presents a unique way to describe your family.

A family theme is the vision statement you both make for your marriage, which trickles down to your family. It has lots of benefits, with one benefit being a common goal for your marriage and family to work towards. We like to sum this up in one or two words as a common theme that guides all our choices and the decisions we make.

In order to choose your family theme, you both need to know and agree on what you want your family to exemplify or be portrayed as. For us, we chose *Peaceful Family*. We wanted our home to be inviting, calm, warm, and happy. The word "peaceful" summed up our goals. We decided how many social events we would go to every month based on if it would create a peaceful atmosphere or a busy atmosphere. As a result, we keep a balanced calendar each month.

Health was important to us having a peaceful home, therefore, clean eating is a top priority for our household. Debt and money fights are the opposite of a peaceful home, so we are working on paying off our debt. We pay cash for everything we can afford or wait to purchase it. Budgeting every month with weekly marriage check-ups is a norm for us too.

A family theme provides your marriage with direction and cohesiveness. It acts as a guide to your marriage so you can check in and see if you are meeting your goals or if you need to adjust something.

In fifty years what do you want your marriage and home atmosphere to be remembered as? What about your legacy? One of the best moments about having a family theme is when people describe your family as your family theme. We love to hear friends, relatives, and even strangers call our family peaceful since our family theme is peaceful family.

I vividly remember when a complete stranger approached us at a country store the year after we were married just to tell us we send out a peaceful loving vibe. That was certainly proof that having a family theme can positively impact other lives. – Ashley

Imagine if instead of our family it was your family? How would you feel?

Due to the success we have had with our family theme, we want to share it with you. It has certainly helped us to build a strong foundation and improved our marriage, especially in how relate with each other. We have compiled the steps we took in choosing our family theme into six simple sections that you can practice today.

How to Choose a Family Theme

Step 1: Understand Family Themes

Choosing a family theme played a very big role for us having a peaceful family. This family theme is not an aspiration that we set for the New Year, it is the theme for our family and everyday life. Our theme is very simple, but also a profound guidance for every decision we make. Therefore we invested some days in picking ours.

We believe that once our marriage and family is peaceful, all other endeavors we pursue will yield better results. A simple family theme will not only impact your marriage and family positively, but it will also be the yardstick to determine if your family should pursue certain endeavors or not.

If you and your spouse do not have a simple family theme that you both agree, and are committed to accomplishing, you should invest some time this week to choose one for your family.

It could simply be being a debt free family, a peaceful family, a hardworking family, a giving family, etc.

Pick something positive that you wish your life to reflect in your marriage, family, and home, which by default will transcend into your environment and outside your home.

Step 2: Define Your "Why" For Your Family Theme

Are you ready? If you are, then grab a pen or pencil and a sheet of paper; this section involves brainstorming. Kindly go through this section with your spouse, answer each question and write down all your answers. At the end of each question, we share our answer to provide you with a better understanding of the question.

1. Write down all the words that you think best describes your marriage, family and life you want. Do you see a common theme?

2. Why do you want this theme for your marriage and family?

   We want our marriage and home to be known as peaceful, nurturing, and loving.

3. Why will a family theme be so important for you and your spouse?

   It will enable us to provide a great environment for us to live together, grow, and learn with our children. It also sets the tone and temperament for every choice and response we make as a couple.

4. Why do you believe in this theme?

To put it lightly, we love living a stress-free life and our family theme enables us to do so. In addition, we believe wherever peace exists there is unity, productivity level increases, almost everything becomes easier, plus our inner joy escalates.

I love living a chaos-free lifestyle, little to no stress if possible and simply enjoying a quiet peaceful home. I have always tried to live this way since it protects me from avoidable events. This does not imply I do not take risks; I enjoy the thrills of taking calculated risks.

As a result, choosing a family theme was not difficult for us since we shared similar ideas and knew what we wanted our future family to be. It was only through our brainstorming *section, and understanding our **why**, that we agreed to choose "Peaceful" for our family theme.* – Marcus

I believe having a family theme is such an integral part of any family. Someone with goals has that push to always improve him or herself and move forward does just that. An individual without goals just kind of wanders through life. The reason why this theme is so important to me is because of my childhood.

Before I became a wife and mother, I was the total opposite: my life was always filled with high stress, unbalanced and unpredictable things. By choosing a theme for our family, I have comfort as a wife, knowing my husband and I are working together as a team to provide a nurturing and an encouraging home for our children. – Ashley

Did you notice the words Ashley uses to describe how she views a *peaceful* family and the words Marcus used?

Remember, you both speak different languages; see where your ideas connect, and go from there.

Step 3: Why Is "Why" Important For Your Family Theme?

We found a very enlightening and inspiring TED video, "Start with Why", by Simon Sinek to watch. (You can watch this video at: www.ourpeacefulfamily.com/simonsinek). This video will help you further understand your *Why*. Simon Sinek shows us with excellent and simple to understand examples about starting with your *Why*.

It is one of the best TED videos you would ever invest a few minutes of your life watching and the return on investment is amazing. Once you are done watching the video, please answer the three questions again, and make corrections if needed.

1. Why do you want this theme for your family?

2. Why will a family theme be so important for you and your spouse?

3. Why do you believe in this family theme?

We have personally watched Simon Sinek's TED video and both believe you should not miss it. The lesson we learned from this video helped us to clearly define our reason for making certain decisions, choices, setting goals (in this case choosing a theme for our marriage and family), starting a business etc. In this video, Simon Sinek gives such a great example on why it is so important to have a main belief, goal, or *why* for a business. This lesson is just as important and should be applied to other areas of our lives; like our marriage and family.

In just the first seven minutes, he explains the *golden circle* and the trickle effect. An example that's close to home for us would be:

» We want a peaceful lifestyle

» How do we have a peaceful life style?

» The core of why we want a peaceful lifestyle.

Simon explains this system is backwards and we should think C, B, A instead of A, B, C. Does that make sense to you?

Why should we have a theme for our marriage and family? For us it is to have a peaceful family to enjoy life, raise responsible and amazing individuals, and living life at the absolute fullest. Then we lay out our ground rules, boundaries, and put systems in place to help us structure our how.

Lastly, the results from our theme are a warm inviting home, with minimal stress, and no fighting. This explanation is just an example that we hope you find helpful on your journey to choosing your own family theme.

Did Sinek's video enable you and your spouse to rethink your *why* and come out with better answers?

Step 4: Family Theme Actionable Steps

You and your spouse should at least have an idea about what your family theme should be if not already chosen. The goals you have for your marriage and family. Have you thought about some of the benefits of choosing this theme/lifestyle that you foresee? What will the positive impacts of your chosen theme have on yourself, your spouse, children, relatives, and society?

For our theme, the positive impacts included but are not limited to: inner joy, great environment for family bonding, effective communication, people feeling very relaxed at our home, and learning from us.

Turning Your Theme Into Reality

Choosing a theme is the first step towards creating the vision for your marriage and family. The second and most important step is to practice the daily activities that will make your vision a reality. To do that, answer the questions below with your spouse.

1. What do both of you need to do to everyday to accomplish your family theme?

   For us, we fight fair and lessen our disagreements through effective communication.

2. When do you want to see the results of your family theme?

A maximum of 6 months into your marriage, but we saw results much sooner. We decided on 6 months since you should see improvement by then. If you do not, something is wrong somewhere and you should re-evaluate where you can make changes.

3. How will you hold each other accountable towards making your family theme a reality?

   We both ensure our home is clean and organized, as much as possible with two little ones. We limit how busy we get and go over our calendar together. Learning to fight fair and communicating effectively helps us create a peaceful environment. In addition, we asked each other questions about our family theme, especially whether we were headed in the right direction.

4. How do you want to achieve your family theme?

   List the steps to achieving your goal. Create a plan of action! Laugh and smile often, hug and kiss before leaving home for work, etc., communicate to ensure everything is fine at home, decorate our home accordingly, be patient, and make it a priority to have a peaceful family.

Some of the results and benefits we experienced after going through the above action steps was less stress and chaos at home. We also saw an increase in productivity with work since either one of us leaves home happily and knows we will come back to a peaceful home. In addition, always remember the benefits of your family theme since it will increase your desire to make it a reality.

Remember, your family theme must be specific (simple), measurable (how will its results or progress be measured), attainable (can it be done, is it actionable), realistic (real not vague or something impossible like a perfect family, no one is perfect), and time bound (when should the theme be seen by others, or reflect your family actions, image, etc.)

The best way to predict your future is to create it.

– Stephen Covey

Our Family Theme

As a couple, we believe it is essential to have simple common goals for your marriage and family. We decided that having a peaceful family was one of our goals for the kind of home we would like to have and raise our children in.

Communication, hand in hand partnership, working together as a team not against each other, agreeing on finances and lots of patience are some of the skills we use to make this happen. We wanted this peaceful family theme for our home because of our future goals and past experiences. Plus we did not want to repeat some of our past family experiences, or even let our children go through them.

We quickly realized the best option moving forward was to identify what our past was, what our present is and what we want our future to be. We both had different upbringing therefore by identifying our differences, we were able to choose our family theme.

Due to my upbringing, I didn't know how to properly disagree. I was very quick tempered and had no patience the first year we were married. Slowly and painfully, I swallowed my pride and took the steps required to work on these things; as well as the insecurities that popped up.

What helped us survive our first year of marriage was my husband being incredibly patient and understanding with me. – Ashley

*I had to learn to understand where she was coming from. I needed to loosen up, listen attentively to her needs and not be rigid due to my vastly different upbringing. Whenever we talk about our first year of marriage, I tell my wife honestly that if she hadn't changed and improved herself, we would probably be divorced because neither of us wants to **live** an unhappy life. She agrees, as we both have done a lot of growing and changing.* – Marcus

By working together as a team, trusting each other, listening to each other's healthy critiques, planning, sharing duties and responsibilities, and organizing our home we were able to build a solid foundation for our marriage.

In addition, we have joint bank accounts, budget monthly, agree on our children's upbringing, respect each other, read at least one marriage or family book together each year, plan yearly goals for our family, try to enjoy every moment of our daily family time together, and believe that everything will work out fine; this helps us to minimize the stress on ourselves and our marriage.

The awesome result of choosing a family theme has enabled us to connect and grow together over the past few years in our marriage while nurturing our peaceful marriage and family. We believe you can have a peaceful marriage and family too, especially if that is the theme you choose. If you need help choosing one, send us a message and we will be glad to help you come up with a theme that is integral and vital to your family's aspirations.

Yearly goal setting is essential in keeping you both on track to maintain your family theme as well as progressing together. At the end of the year we sit down together and go over all the goals we have for our spiritual, educational, relational, social, wellness, family, and financial aspects of our marriage and life together. We have our own separate personal goals, but this list is for our life together. We make a list on a paper and hang it up in our office so we can see it all year round to make sure we are on track.

Usually at the 6-month mark we look it over together and see what we need to improve on to make those goals a reality. This was a tradition we started the first year we were married and have continued since. It helps us talk about all the big purchases we need to make, as well as all these other important goals giving us a chance to talk and get all of it out in the open. We agree on these goals and work together to make them happen. We believe yearly goal setting will benefit your marriage and help you grow together to achieve the family theme and goals you have set (or will set) for your family.

Chapter 11

The Choice Is Yours

Treat a man as he is and he will remain as he is. Treat a man as he can and should be and he will become as he can and should be.

– Stephen R. Covey

The first year of marriage is very important as it sets the foundation for the rest of your marriage. Be very open about sharing your thoughts, feelings, and opinions so you do not build resentment over time. A happy, healthy, and fulfilling marriage does not happen overnight. It takes time, effort, and intentionality from both husband and wife.

As you know, a critical component in building a house is setting the foundation. It also determines whether the house will be stable or not, collapse in X number of years, and how long it will last. The foundation is built with extreme care because without it the house will eventually cease to exist.

If we extremely value the foundation for a house, why don't we value the setting of a strong foundation for our marriage and family? As newlyweds, you and your spouse must use your first year to intentionally build a strong foundation for the marriage you both dreamed about.

Most of the marriage issues that couples face relate to intimacy, trust, faith, love, respect, sex, communication, finances, and commitment. You could also add family goals, extended families, in-laws, career, children, and the unexpected life events that occur.

We believe if the foundation for every marriage is built right and kept strong, especially in the first year, the marriage will be able to withstand and avoid most of the problems that lead to divorce. By practicing what you have learned from this book in your marriage today, you will have a marriage and family that grows stronger and positively impacts society.

There will be some challenges with the adjustments that come from being engaged to being married but do not be afraid. Enjoy your first year, learn, grow together, and remember why you got married in the first place.

We hope this book helps you and your spouse to have a great first year of marriage with our advice and that it helps you to build a strong foundation for the healthy, happy, successful, and lasting marriage you desire.

Set the sail of your marriage by practicing the information in this book today.

The following questions are will help you talk, connect, and know each other at a deeper level. Discuss them to unveil some of your unspoken marriage expectations. Take some time, grab some paper and a pen to sit down and go through a few questions a night together.

Relational Expectations Questions to Discuss

» Is there anything I do that causes you to question my love for you?

» How can I show you that I love you?

» If I was unable to have children for a medical reason, how would that affect our marriage?

» Which of these statements best describes your understanding of love:

- Never having to say you're sorry.

- Always having to say you're sorry.

- Being the first to say I'm sorry.

» Which events from your childhood influence your behavior, choices and attitude the most?

» If you meet an ex, do you think you could rekindle any romantic feelings for them even though you are married to me?

» Is there anything in your past I need to know about?

» What is the biggest thing you didn't like about your previous girlfriend/boyfriend?

» If you asked your ex to list your top three worst characteristics, what would they be?

» Do you keep anything your ex gave you? Why or why not?

» Would you be okay to continue our marriage if there are things in my past that I am not ready or willing to talk you about right now?

» Have you ever done anything illegal? What was it?

» Were either of your parents abusive to you or each other in any way? (Physical, emotional, sexual or verbal.)

» What was your parent's attitude towards marriage and how has it affected you?

» What is one bad habit you have been able to overcome?

» Have you ever been in an abusive relationship?

» What is one time you were uncomfortable with the way I behaved with another person you thought I may be attracted to, or that was attracted to me.

» What is something I do now, or could do in the future that would make you not trust me?

» Do I have your complete trust or is it something that develops over time?

» Does a spouse always come first, or does the children?

» Is a great career more important than our marriage and family?

» How did your family resolve conflicts when you were growing up? Was that a good method or not? What would you change about the way they resolve conflicts to apply to our marriage?

» Is there anything about marriage that scares you?

» If we were having issues in our marriage, in what order would you ask for help of the following:

    a. Divorce lawyer

    b. Your parents

    c. A sibling

    d. A marriage counselor

    e. Me

    f. A religious leader

    g. A friend

» Why this order?

» How will you help support my interests and hobbies?

» How do you feel about supporting my family financially if ever needed?

» How do you feel about having my parents move in with us if they ever needed to?

» Would you have any regrets about things you couldn't accomplish by you choosing to be married to me?

» Whenever we have feelings of hurt, frustration, annoyance or anger about each other, should we:

    a. Remain silent.

    b. Say something as soon as the feelings arise.

    c. Wait a certain amount of time before raising the issue.

    d. Do something else? If so, what?

» If you always say you are going to do something but never do it, how can I bring this problem to your attention?

» What did you admire about your parents relationship the way your mother and father treated each other?

» What is the best way for me to communicate difficult feelings about you so that you are not offended?

» Who are you okay with knowing about the arguments we have?

» What makes you not want to talk to me?

» Do you feel you could communicate with me under any circumstance and about any subject?

» Rank all the priorities in your life: work, school, family, spouse, friends, hobbies, and spiritual? How much time will you spend on each of these?

» Are you closer to your mother or father? Why?

Social Expectations Questions to Discuss

Early on in our marriage, we discovered that one of us was an introvert and the other an extrovert. We had to communicate our desires and expectations to come up with a compromise.

» How often do you want to go to social events each month?

» How often do you want your spouse to join you? Now come up with a compromise that you can both live with.

» How often will you go out on dates with your spouse each month?

» Do you prefer a set daily schedule or flexible activities and timetables?

» How often will you have a girls/guys night?

» Do you plan on spending as much time with your friends, work, family and entertainment activities after we are married as much as you do now as a single person? Why or why not?

» Would you prefer to live in the country or city? Why?

» If I had to move away from our families for a better job opportunity, would you support that decision?

» How would you feel if I had to travel a lot to see family, work, or hobby?

» How will we schedule holidays with our families?

Household Expectations Questions to Discuss

» Who will do what as far as chores are concerned?

» Will you alternate the house chores?

» How clean do you want your house to be?

» What kind of food will you eat?

» Who will cook, and when?

» Who does the grocery list and meal planning?

» Who takes the trash out?

» Who maintains the cars?

» What role do you play in a marriage?

» What is your spouse's role?

» When did you begin to form these ideas of roles?

» What does the word marriage mean to you?

» What does the word love mean to you?

» What is something you want to emulate from your parents or marriage role models relationship?

» What is something you don't want in your marriage from theirs?

» Where are your strengths? Weakness?

» What are our biggest differences? Could this cause future conflict? How do our differences complement each other?

» How can you specifically apply your strengths and balance your weaknesses in your marriage?

» How would you treat stepchildren?

» How do you plan on raising our children?

    a. The same way you were raised.

    b. Completely differently from the way you were raised.

    c. A mixture of both.

» How long do you want to be married before we have children?

» What type of school would you like our children to be taught in? (Montessori, Waldorf, homeschool, traditional public school, private school, un-school, etc.)

» If we have children who will be changing the diapers, feeding the babies in the middle of the night, bathing, taking the child to the doctor, shopping for the child, etc.?

» What type of discipline would you use? What types of discipline are you absolutely not okay with?

» If we have a boy, do you want him circumcised?

» When you want to have kids?

Annoyances and Quirks Questions to Discuss

» If I had bad breath, body odor, running makeup, or wear dirty clothes, will you tell me? Should I tell you? Why or why not? How should we do it?

» What is nagging to you? Do you feel like I nag you ever? How does it make you feel when I nag you?

» Do you like the way I dress?

» What does my family do that annoys, frustrates and makes you angry?

» Is there anything you do in your career that I would be hurt about or disapprove of?

» Do you believe that you should stay married if you are unhappy all the time?

» When do you need space away from me?

Miscellaneous Questions to Discuss

» What are some things you are afraid of?

» What influence, if any, do you believe my family should have on our marriage?

» Do you believe that our parents should know our financial situation, whether it is good or bad? How far should this go?

» What are your views on pornography?

» How would you react if our son or daughter told us they were gay or transgender?

» How do you feel about having guns in our home?

» Is there anyone close to you who feels we should not be married? Why?

» What health problems do you have?

» Have you ever had any psychological problems?

» When you are in a bad mood, how should I deal with it?

» Do you want to have pets? How many?

» How do you define cheating or infidelity?

» What to do if we find out our unborn child has disability?

» Birth control methods?

» Will you go to marriage counseling if I ask you to?

» What will you do if you thought our marriage was failing?

» How will we resolve issues we disagree on?

» What political party do you support?

» What are your deal breakers?

» Where do you want to live?

» What role does our extended family play in our family?

» What happens if one person changes their spiritual beliefs?

» What retirement plans do you have?

» What kind of rules do you want to establish for our marriage?

» How much time will you spend on your phone when you are with me?

» How much time will you spend watching TV or media every day?

» Toilet seat up or down?

» Is it okay to have a relationship with an ex?

Monetary Expectations Questions to Discuss

A few questions to consider on how to agree on finances in marriage or money related issues with your spouse include:

» Do you trust me with money?

» When to buy a house?

» How will you spend your money?

» Are you comfortable putting all our money together and sharing an account?

» Will you use credit cards?

» What is your credit score?

» What kind of things will you buy?

» What kind of things won't you buy?

» What kind of material lifestyle will you have?

» How much will you spend on groceries a week/month?

» How much will you spend on personal blow money?

» How often will you eat out?

» Is it okay to purchase an item for $100 without talking to your spouse?

» What circumstances are you okay with going into debt for?

» How much debt do you personally owe including any student loans, credit cards, family loans, etc.?

» Do you feel stressed when dealing with financial issues? How do you deal with that stress?

» How often do you use credit cards and what do you buy with them?

» How many credit cards do you have and what are their balances?

» How should we prepare for a financial emergency?

» Do you think that not having enough money is a good reason not to have children?

» If we have children will you or I stay home with the child or will they go to daycare? For how long?

» Will we have a budget every month?

» How do you feel about helping me pay off my debt?

» How do you feel about saving money? How much do you think we should be saving every month? What are we saving for?

» Do you prefer bank accounts separate and assets in different names? Why or why not?

» What retirement plans do you have?

» What insurances do you have? Health, Auto, Life, Disability, Homeowners etc.

» Do you have any investments?

» Do you plan on investing? How so?

» Who is the saver or spender?

» What marriage expectations do you have when it comes to how you will handle finances?

» Who balances the checkbook?

» How do either one of you view money? Is it bad? Is it a tool? Is it only for a select few of people?

» What are your financial goals? Do you want just enough to pay your bills and have some money to spend on whatever you want?

» Do you want to pay off our house early?

» What do you want your life to look like in 10-20-50 years financially?

» Why is agreeing on finances or budgeting important to you?

Sexual Questions to Discuss Together

» In marriage, sex is?

» On a scale of 1-10 how important is sex in marriage?

» What is the minimum amount of times you want to have sex in a week?

» Describe how you feel about sex.

» How do you feel about your body?

» How do you want to express your love through physical affection?

» How do you want your spouse to express their affection for you?

» What fears or concerns do you have about sex?

» What do you look forward to in your marriage sexually?

» Do you feel sexually connected and safe?

» How would you define a sexless marriage?

» What turns you on?

» What turns you off?

» Where do you crave to be touched before, during and after sex?

» What sex acts do you find off limits or consider gross?

» What are your sexual fantasies or sex acts you have always wanted to try?

» What is your favorite sex position?

» What is your/your spouse's role during sex?

» Is there anything that happened or certain attitudes about sex from your childhood that affects how you view sex?

» Is there anything you believe your spouse should know to better understand you sexually?

» What must we do if one of us does not want sex?

» What must we do when we fight about sex? How should we handle it?

» What happens if I am not in the mood to have sex?

» When we experience health issues like menopause, erectile dysfunction, pain during sex, hormonal changes due to childbirth, etc. what should we do?

» If you take away our physical attraction to each other, what would be remaining?

» How will it affect our sexual relationship if I gain weight?

***If you have been sexually assaulted in anyway, it would be very helpful and possibly healing for you to discuss those things with your spouse; if you feel safe.

Thank you

Congratulations on reading this far! We are very thankful and excited to help you build a strong foundation for your marriage.

If you enjoyed reading this book, please leave us a review on Amazon and share the book with other couples. We would both love to know how this book impacts you and your marriage and what we can do to make it better.

You can also send us an email about any questions you have about adjusting to married life to firstyearmarriage@ gmail.com.

We cannot promise that we will immediately reply every email due to the volume of emails we receive, but we will do our best to cover your question in future blog posts or podcast episodes.

If you would like to receive email updates about future books, bonuses, plus get your FREE 12-Week action plan, visit the website below today:

www.ourpeacefulfamily.com/12weekactionplan

Thank you again for choosing and reading our book!

Marcus and Ashley Kusi
Enjoy your marriage, enjoy your life!

Other Books by Marcus and Ashley

» *Communication in Marriage: How to Communicate with Your Spouse Without Fighting*

» *My Tandem Nursing Journey: Breastfeeding Through Pregnancy, Labor, Nursing Aversion and Beyond*

Excellent Resources

If you have not yet read the books below, we highly recommend you get a copy from your local library or buy one online.

1. The Five Love Languages by Dr. Gary Smalley.
2. Love and Respect by Dr. Emerson Eggerichs.
3. Boundaries In Marriage by Dr. Henry Cloud.
4. Boundaries by Dr. Henry Cloud.
5. 48 Days to The Work You Love by Dan Miller.
6. The Total Money Makeover by Dave Ramsey.
7. QBQ: The Question Behind The Question by John Miller.

You should also check out the list of excellent marriage resources we recommend for couples by visiting our website below:

www.ourpeacefulfamily.com/resources

Lastly, listen to the *First Year Marriage* podcast at the website below to learn from the first year marriage experiences of other amazing couples:

www.firstyearmarriage.com

References

Cloud, Henry, and John Sims Townsend. *Boundaries in Marriage*. Grand Rapids, MI: ZondervanPublishingHouse, 1999. Print.

"Divorce Statistics." *Information on Divorce Rate Statistics*. Web. 18 May 2016.

About Marcus and Ashley

We help overwhelmed newlyweds adjust to married life and inspire married couples to improve their marriage so they can become better husbands and wives.

We do this by using our own marriage experience, that of great married couples, and sharing what works for us through our website and marriage podcast, *The First Year Marriage Show*.

Visit the website below to listen to the podcast.
www.firstyearmarriage.com

Visit our website to learn more about us.
www.ourpeacefulfamily.com

Marriage is a life-long journey that thrives on love, commitment, trust, respect, communication, patience, and companionship.

– Ashley and Marcus Kusi

Made in the USA
Lexington, KY
30 March 2017